More Praise for *Active Faith*

"This timely book helps Christians in the Wesleyan tradition think about how to respond to divisive issues in church and society that are fueled by persistent misunderstandings of our faith. Drawing from scripture and tradition, Chilcote offers insight into how to open ourselves to the guidance of the Holy Spirit to put love into practice as witness to the love we know in Jesus Christ. This is an important study for all who want to gain the mind of Christ in order to resist the dangerous distortions of faith all around us."

—Sarah Heaner Lancaster, Werner Professor of Theology, Methodist Theological School in Ohio, Delaware, OH

"Through scripture and stories, Paul Chilcote invites us on a journey with him as he discusses the dangerous ideologies of fundamentalism, nationalism, dispensationalism, and antinomianism and the havoc they continue to wreak on Christian faith and practice. He challenges the descendants of John and Charles Wesley to take seriously our Wesleyan spiritual tradition and to practice the spiritual disciplines of humility, hospitality, healing, and holiness. This is a timely and inspiring book from a United Methodist theologian, calling us—individuals and congregations—to a time of reflection and conversation as we discern what it means to live an active faith worthy of the Wesleyan heritage toward a betterment of our church and world."

—Kah-Jin Jeffrey Kuan, president and professor of Hebrew Bible, Claremont School of Theology, Claremont, CA; elder, California-Nevada Annual Conference, UMC

Other Abingdon Press Books to Consider

Holy Love, Steve Harper

Paul W. Chilcote

ACTIVE FAITH

Resisting
4 Dangerous Ideologies
with the Wesleyan Way

✝ I Abingdon Press™
Nashville

ACTIVE FAITH:
RESISTING 4 DANGEROUS IDEOLOGIES WITH THE WESLEYAN WAY

Copyright © 2019 by Abingdon Press

All rights reserved.

Library of Congress Control Number: 2019948946

ISBN: 978-1-791-00172-8

19 20 21 22 23 24 25 26 27 28 29—10 9 8 7 6 5 4 3 2 1
MANUFACTURED IN THE UNITED STATES OF AMERICA

In memory of
Hugh Price Hughes, Forward Movement founder
Georgia Harkness, Personalist theologian of peace
And in honor of
Peter Storey, South African activist for truth and reconciliation
All models of active faith

CONTENTS

PREFACE

I want a life filled with truth, joy, peace, and love. I pray you do too. I see these qualities in Jesus, and I have seen them lived out in the active faith of others. So I know this is possible. The question is, how do you find a way forward into such a life? This is both a personal question and a question for the community of faith. In this quest for authenticity, both ideas and practices are important. "Practice what you preach," we say, and the statement itself bears witness to the fact that this is not easy. Truth be told, you can never really separate how you think about things from how you act. A "chicken and egg" mutuality holds these things together. Ideas shape our behavior, and practices shape the way we think. Ideas require reflection; actions entail resolve.

God is again stirring up active faith in many communities. I witnessed this in the United Methodist Annual Conference sessions during the spring of 2019. This is not to say that putting love into faithful action is a new thing. This is far from the case. I would actually argue that this is one of the gold threads that has always been an important part of the Wesleyan tradition from the very beginning. John and Charles Wesley insisted that active faith characterizes authentic discipleship. Conditions in the life of the church and our world have stirred this up again. Faithfully living out the love of Jesus requires energy, and the Holy Spirit is the primary source of spiritual energy. So I view these new developments as something Spirit-breathed. This rediscovery of active faith entails a renewed sense of hope. Those who long for a way forward see God doing a new thing, and this gets them excited. All day long God is at work for good. I interpret the wave sweeping through the church as a good work of God, a life-giving event, an in-breaking of God's way and rule.

While this progressive Wesleyan movement is proactive, it also represents a reaction against some concurrent developments.[1] In particular, active faith reacts against four dangerous ideological insurgencies. These movements associated with more conservative forms of Protestantism have captured minds and hearts, not only in Methodism but across the broad spectrum of the church. The breathtakingly rapid changes in culture, and the rise of fear related to them, explain the rise of these ideologies in large measure. But some have been around for a long time. Fundamentalism, nationalism, and antinomianism, for example, can be traced back easily to the times in which the Bible was written. They are perennial. Dispensationalism, on the other hand, is relatively new. In American culture, however, it pervades evangelical Christianity.

In this book I will explain each of these in clear and understandable terms. I'm not so much concerned about their origins as their effects. So I will also point out their dangers and describe a progressive Wesleyan perspective as an alternative, biblical way— the way of Jesus. I believe a church that reflects the values of humility, hospitality, healing, and holiness pleases God. When we practice these spiritual disciplines—active faith—we rediscover truth, joy, peace, and love.

I dedicated this brief book to three of my heroes. I think of them as exemplars of the progressive Wesleyan spirit. Hugh Price Hughes founded the Forward Movement to reshape the Wesleyan Methodist Church as the moral and social conscience of Britain in the nineteenth century. Georgia Harkness served as the first woman professor in a theological seminary in the United States. As an evangelical liberal theologian in the tradition of Boston Personalism, she advocated for the full inclusion of women in ministry and the dignity of all persons. Peter Storey, a Methodist pastor and ecumenical leader in South Africa, resisted the racist apartheid regime and participated in the subsequent restorative justice processes of the Truth and Reconciliation Commission. Each of these followers of Jesus translated their love of God and others into faithful action. Together, they model for me the way of a progressive Wesleyan—a way of active faith.

Paul W. Chilcote
July 31, 2019, St. Ignatius of Loyola Day

Prologue

PRACTICING A WAY FORWARD TOGETHER

I never thought I would publish a declaration—a manifesto. I never contemplated the idea that a situation would push me so far as to compel me to articulate a statement about it. I have always tended to work more quietly in the background. But I feel compelled to respond to the current state of affairs, both in the church and in society, with a declaration. I hope you don't interpret this manifesto as a battle cry. I confess it might feel like that to some. But I am weary of combat, and I know that is not the way forward. I long for a Christian witness in our world that is perceived as something other than judgmental, hypocritical, and hateful. I would love for others to witness the church at work and say, "My goodness, they really do love one another and everyone else!" My primary interest lies in speaking the truth in love for the sake of God's mission of love in the world.

"When in the course of human events it becomes necessary..." You recognize these as the opening words of the American Declaration of Independence, probably the best-known declaration to all of us. In my view, we have reached that point. Perhaps my sense of urgency comes from the perception that a shadow hovers over the life of the church and the world. I have spoken to countless people, old and young, who feel like this. I long for the wind of the Holy Spirit to blow away the clouds in which we are engulfed. While I know that God is always at work for good in the world and is laying out a future filled with hope before us, I want to feel this more deeply in my bones. I am also convinced that practices, more than ideas, will help us find a way forward into the brightness of God's grace. Little steps can lead to major changes. The Wesleyan heritage offers us amazing gifts in this regard.

So what is a "progressive Wesleyan declaration," and how can we find a way forward by practicing the way of Jesus, as rediscovered by the Wesleys?

Over the past year or so I have embraced increasingly the term *progressive Wesleyan*. *Pro* means forward and *grad* (the Latin term from which *gress* is derived) means step. In this book I invite you to step forward. Today we might say "lean into" a future of truth, joy, peace, and love that God intends for all people. My hope is that we can all "graduate," that is, take our next step together. Wesleyan Christians stand in a heritage of love divine that is deep, broad, high, and lengthy. I have no interest in resurrecting John and Charles Wesley simply for the sake of being a good Methodist; rather, I find in them compelling mentors in the Christian faith. They provided a deep spiritual well for us, and we have the opportunity to draw from it.

This book is not so much about answering questions as it is about finding a way forward together. Obviously, this is not a new concept or concern for Methodists. I, for one, was deeply moved by the prayerful, sensitive, and discerning work of the

Commission on a Way Forward over the course of its two-year life span. On the recommendation of the Council of Bishops, the United Methodist General Conference of 2016 established this international team to explore options that help to maintain and strengthen the unity of the church. Most people realized, I am sure, that the pressing issue of human sexuality was only one of a number of issues threatening to divide the church. Despite their good work, we continue in the struggle to find a way forward. Rather than discouraging us, however, we need to remind ourselves that we have always been "on the way." The idea of pilgrimage or journey has always been deeply embedded in our Wesleyan DNA.

One reason I decided to write this book is my fear that many Christians today have succumbed, perhaps unwittingly, to seductive ideas that distort the Christian message and threaten to compromise our witness to the love of Jesus in the world. This is my judgment, and I own it. Ideas and attitudes can be dangerous. Some appeal to our base instincts, and in times of anxiety and stress, such ideas can lead us in the wrong direction. So I believe we must confront false claims directly and with honesty but in love.

I am not a fan of "isms." I prefer to engage real persons, not ideas. But in a declaration of this nature, some abstractions and generalizations are necessary. Regardless, I don't want us to forget about real people in real-life situations. I will tell such stories too. Jesus loved people more than ideas, and this is the approach I want to embrace as well. It is, in fact, essential to the way of Jesus.

My immediate concern revolves around four movements that are prevalent or surging in our time and affect private and corporate conceptions of the Christian faith.

The "Christian" fundamentalist, for example, claims to possess all the truth above all other claims. We find the truth, however, through the posture of humility, by elevating others rather than ourselves.

The "Christian" nationalist believes that his or her tribe is superior to all others. But we find joy when we make room for and welcome others through our hospitality, when we embrace the diversity that surrounds us.

The "Christian" dispensationalist focuses attention on the "otherworldly" aspects of religious life, drawing attention away from God's call to steward this earth and care for the world. We find peace, however, when we participate in God's restoration of all things in processes of healing.

The "Christian" antinomian truncates the gospel, emphasizing faith rather than love as the goal toward which our life in Christ moves. But we find the true meaning of love when we strive to practice a holiness of heart and life characterized by the fullest possible love of God and others.

While this book must be about ideas, in part, it is also about practices. My hope is that conversation around ideas will create a pathway for you into practicing the way of Jesus. I am more convinced than ever that, whereas ideas tend to divide people, practices shape communities and unify them by giving attention to a common goal. Every summer I co-lead a Wesley Pilgrimage to England, and I have always found this to be the case in our experience as we engage in an intentional journey together. Our pilgrims, most of them provisional candidates for the ministry who are drawn often from more than twenty annual conferences, bond with one another in the corporate disciplines in which we engage. Despite the different seminaries at which they have trained or the regions of the country or world from which they have come, praying unites us all. Gathering together around the Lord's Table makes us one. Immersing ourselves in the Word of God leads to an appreciation of our unity-in-diversity, as does conversation in the context of small groups. Singing the hymns of our faith binds our hearts as brothers and sisters in one family.

In this study I invite you to practice the way of Jesus by engaging in four formative practices that represent central themes related to the progressive Wesleyan way. They function as counterpoints to the four dangers I've introduced above. I consider these enacted practices to be acts of resistance against these ideologies. They align with Wesleyan theology and spirituality. They gave direction to the communities of faith organized and directed by the Wesley brothers. Moreover, they fueled early Methodism as a movement of spiritual renewal. These practices revolve around the words *humility*, *hospitality*, *healing*, and *holiness*. I relate each of these practices to the quest for a particular virtue as well, namely, *truth*, *joy*, *peace*, and *love*.

In each of the four chapters that follow, then, I discuss the relationship of these practices to scripture, identifying a signature biblical text or story related to each. I introduce you to the work of spiritual mentors who can help you understand and embrace the practice more fully. I describe contemporary forms of Christianity that distort or compromise Jesus's way as it relates to the practices, primarily as a consequence of fear. I direct your attention to a contemporary issue in which these ideological insurgencies figure prominently and in which a progressive Wesleyan perspective offers an alternative vision of Christian authenticity. Finally, I offer practical guidance with regard to how you can engage in these practices.

Declarations draw attention to the need for change. They emerge at critical turning points. They celebrate the possibility of new discoveries and new lived realities. For the community of faith, they often promote the vision of a future filled with hope and love. That is my hope with regard to this book. The prophet Isaiah provided one of the most important declarations of all time in a promise of God related to restoration and protection: "I'm doing a new thing; now it sprouts up; don't you recognize it? I'm making a way in the desert, paths in the wilderness (Isa 43:19 CEB). I hope and pray that this progressive Wesleyan declaration opens new horizons and possibilities for you as you practice humility, hospitality, healing, and holiness. You can do this on your own or in the context of a small group. I invite you to pray for an open heart and an open mind so that God, through us all, might open our doors more fully.

Chapter One

TRUTH AND THE PRACTICE OF HUMILITY

Some experiences you never forget. I was auditing a class on Howard Thurman as a student at Duke Divinity School. Thurman had been one of the main influences on Martin Luther King Jr. About halfway through the semester, the students were sitting in our small seminar room, waiting for class to begin. The door opened and Howard Thurman walked into the room. Our professor, Herb Edwards, had surprised us royally. It was as though someone turned on the lights. Thurman radiated God's love. I will never forget that moment. In addition to his radiant countenance, I remember his deep humility. He communicated humility by the way he related to each of us. He acted as though we were more important than he was. He expressed interest in getting to know each of us. It was as though he was visiting our class because he felt privileged to share time with us. The topic of discussion was simply "truth," and he revealed something quite profound to me that day. He demonstrated how relationships—and particularly the posture we assume in our relationships in life—shape our truth. I still remember him saying something to the effect that the ultimate test of your truth is the humility that it inspires.

Humility is evident when lifting other people up. The most important truths in life emerge from relationships of mutual submission and genuine appreciation. Progressive Wesleyans assume a posture of humble service in relation to others.

Humility in Philippians 2:5-11

Jesus assumed a posture of humility. He showed how this disposition or virtue of humility is profoundly relational. It functions as the primary building block of the Christian life. In his letter to the Philippians, therefore, St. Paul reminds the community to imitate the Christ of whom they sang in one of the earliest hymns of the church:

Adopt the attitude that was in Christ Jesus:

Though he was in the form of God,
    he did not consider being equal with God something to exploit.
But he emptied himself
    by taking the form of a slave
    and by becoming like human beings.
When he found himself in the form of a human,
    he humbled himself by becoming obedient to the point of death,
    even death on a cross.
Therefore, God highly honored him and
    gave hima name above all names,
so that at the name of Jesus everyone
    in heaven, on earth, and under the earth might bow
    and every tongue confess
        that Jesus Christ is Lord, to the glory of God the Father.
(Phil 2:5-11 CEB)

St. Paul's introduction to the hymn establishes the relational dynamics exemplified by Christ.

Therefore, if there is any encouragement in Christ, any comfort in love, any sharing in the Spirit, any sympathy, complete my joy by thinking the same way, having the same love, being united, and agreeing with each other. Don't do anything for selfish purposes, but with humility think of others as better than yourselves. Instead of each person watching out for their own good, watch out for what is better for others. (Phil 2:1-4 CEB)

Humble people relinquish the need to dominate others or to win. They don't wield their power against others. They don't weaponize truth or conceive certainty as the need to be right. Jesus promoted a vision of life in which we find truth by elevating others.

Humility in *The Imitation of Christ*

The devotional classic of Thomas à Kempis, *The Imitation of Christ*, shaped John and Charles Wesley's view of the Christian life profoundly. The theme of humility pervades this spiritual manual for the Christian walk. At the very outset Thomas links a biblical admonition to this central quality of authentic Christian discipleship:

True self-knowledge is the highest and most profitable discovery in life. Do not think of yourself, therefore, more highly than you ought and always think well and highly of others. (I.2)[1]

Thomas prefaces this concluding statement with a radical denunciation of claims to truth that alienate others and sow seeds of division.

If you think you know a lot, acknowledge that there are many more things about which you know nothing. Do not let your knowledge

3

turn you into an arrogant person; rather, admit your own igno-
rance. Those who aspire to be wise seek to nurture a spirit of humility in their lives. (I.2)

Not surprisingly, Thomas counsels against anything that nurtures pride. Pride, he argues, creates an insurmountable barrier
between us and God and us and others. Moreover, since the sin
of pride turns us away from our greatest good, we often need
to be shocked out of our complacency and false sense of self-
importance. Pride "defaces your soul," claims Thomas. "The humble enjoy continuous peace, but envy, anger, and malice fester in
the hearts of the proud" (I.6). This disease must be rooted out at
all costs. It presents the greatest challenge to all who seek to follow
Jesus faithfully. "Always be prepared to battle your pride," Thomas
observes, "for it stands to your left and your right as a perennial
enemy that never rests" (II.9). According to Thomas, however, no
force in the universe is stronger than an intimate relationship with
the God of love, which forms a spirit of humility in the believer.
Love, not truth or knowledge, is the ultimate goal, and in this
regard, Thomas points consistently to the self-giving love of Jesus.

He demonstrates how there is an intimate connection among
grace, gratitude, thanksgiving, and humility. Gratitude and humility, in fact, go hand in hand. You cannot express gratitude to
yourself! When you express gratitude to others, you are demonstrating that relationships define who you are. Gratitude only
happens in relationship to others. Your genuine appreciation for
others, especially those who are different from you, sows the seed
of humility in your life. Whereas pride nurtures hostility, humility cultivates gratitude. The only force potent enough to break

down the barriers of human hostility is the power of divine humility. The humble Lord empties himself of all but love and then, through the power of his love, proclaims peace to those who are far-off (those who are different) as well as to those who are near (his own tribe). Self-emptying love is the way of the progressive Wesleyan Christian.

The Danger of Fundamentalism

I am about to write some things about "Christian" fundamentalism that are far from complimentary. But my mother always taught me to say at least two things that are kind or positive before you ever criticize someone else. And I prefer not to alienate readers who may place themselves in this camp. I aim for honesty here in an effort to understand. I want to be open to change myself and to prepare a pathway for the Spirit to transform us all.

So fundamentalism has a positive purpose because it is an effort to respond to a basic human need—the need for certainty. According to Maslow, in the "hierarchy of needs," human beings require a sense of safety and security in their lives. Certainty helps establish that feeling of security. Fundamentalists also often exhibit a passion and zeal that is commendable, particularly with regard to the lordship of Jesus. All this comes from the depth of the conviction that stirs a fundamentalist. There is nothing "lukewarm" about them. You know where they stand. Not only is this admirable, it is helpful. Clarity often accompanies certainty, and this can help in terms of the quest to understand someone else more fully.

Fundamentalism is not a theology; rather, it is a perspective related to life—a worldview. As such, this term can be applied to and is found in virtually all religions or ideologies. It can also pervade the lives of people all across the political spectrum.

However, the life of a person committed to this viewpoint stands in stark contrast to the portrait of Christian authenticity rooted in humility. The conviction that you possess all the truth—something at the very heart of fundamentalism—not only reflects a human need but also corresponds to a dangerous fear. While needs can have positive value, fear is almost always destructive in nature. All forms of fundamentalism, I think, are rooted in fear—the fear of uncertainty. If we are honest with ourselves, we know that we live more comfortably in a world that is clear-cut and neatly defined. When things are changing rapidly all around us, most of us yearn for something certain, unchanging, stable.

Living in a world that is gray makes most people uneasy. In my experience and probably in yours, however, most of life is not black-and-white. Real life is complex, entangled, and messy. Uncertainty challenges our sense of security. The realization that all things are not certain also challenges our faith. "Religious fundamentalism," concludes Australian historian Paul Collins, "is really an absence of faith—it is a desperate search for absolute certainty."[2] Herein lies the greatest danger. Fundamentalists are driven by this fear. They seek power and control in an effort to preserve an illusion of absolute certainty. A fundamentalist view of the truth almost always leads to a dominant posture in which victory becomes the ultimate goal. But this is so unlike Jesus and the posture he assumes in all his relationships in life.

Other attitudes and behaviors quickly align with fundamentalism in response to this fear. They are equally disturbing and dangerous.

Dogmatism is the tendency to lay down principles as incontrovertibly true, without consideration of evidence or the opinions of others. People who are dogmatic about their beliefs are often the most difficult people with whom to have a conversation. They are averse to genuine dialogue.

Judgmentalism is the tendency to display an excessively critical point of view. All the synonyms related to this term connote a negative or destructive orientation: accusatory, condemnatory, critical, disparaging, faultfinding, severe. The Gospels link this attitude closely with the term *pharisaical*—marked by hypercritical censorious self-righteousness. It should grieve us deeply that recent surveys demonstrate how young people outside the community of faith describe Christians, first and foremost, as people who are judgmental.[3] This is hardly a badge of honor to wear with pride! It does not reflect the way of Jesus.

In our time, the fundamentalist ideology is aligned closely with one particular approach to the Christian scriptures, namely, *biblical literalism* or *biblicism*. Generations of Jesus-followers have read the Bible through multiple interpretive lenses. They have found truth in various levels of meaning in what they also consider to be God's Word. Regardless, a simplistic, literal approach to scripture has taken hold in many circles today. The literalist argues that there is only one meaning to a text and that this truth applies to all times and all situations. A 2011 Gallup Poll indicated that three out of ten Americans interpret the Bible in this way. (Note that the same ideology is applied among "originalists" to the US Constitution.) And this fits well into a mind-set that prefers black-and-white over gray. It creates a sense of certainty, neutralizing the fear that seizes people in a time of change. Not only is this approach to scripture unhelpful, in my view, it is exceedingly dangerous.

The primary danger in this approach is the way in which it conceives truth in static and not dynamic ways. It demands an overly rigid adherence to certain biblical texts or teachings at the expense of context and other scriptural teachings. In his *Case for Traditional Protestantism*, Terry Johnson makes this point in a compelling manner:

> Believers must not fall into an unwarranted Biblicism, which, in the name of biblical authority, narrows the scope of its application to only that which the Bible explicitly states and not to that which it implies as well. This is a danger when the nature of Scripture is not understood. There is not a verse for every occasion. The Bible is not a book of detailed casuistry providing answers for every imaginable ethical question. No doubt some have wished that the Bible were such a book.... Yet it still applies to every occasion. How so? It reveals general principles, which, to be grasped, must be illuminated by the Holy Spirit, and, to be applied concretely in life, must be joined with reason and wisdom. The need of wisdom can be illustrated by this fact—almost all of life is lived between the lines of explicit biblical commands.[4]

The so-called Wesleyan quadrilateral—which views the primacy of scriptural authority in relation to the norms of tradition, reason, and experience—elevates this dynamic view of truth as well.

Contemporary Concerns: The Ministry of Women and LGBTQ+ Kin

The inclusion of women and LGBTQ+ kin in the life of the church are two casualties of biblical literalism in our time.[5] Without question, misogyny and homophobia are on the rise in North American culture, and these perspectives have found their way into the life of the church as well. The harm perpetrated against beloved siblings in the name of Christ, as a consequence of biblical fundamentalism, demands our attention for the sake of Jesus's way. In both instances, literalists marshal a handful of biblical texts to deny these persons a rightful place in the household of God. While it is not possible to provide a thorough examination of the texts, concerns, and arguments here, I want to use these immediate issues to illustrate a progressive Wesleyan approach to these concerns. I believe this perspective entails a healthy and dynamic understanding of truth perceived from a posture of humility.[6]

Fundamentalists argue the prohibition of women in ministry essentially on the literal interpretation of two biblical texts: 1 Timothy 2:12 and 1 Corinthians 14:34. While these two texts, at face value, would seem to prohibit women in ministry, when viewed in context, they do not. "I permit no woman to teach or to have authority over a man," claims the author of 1 Timothy; "she is to keep silent" (1 Tim 2:12 NRSV). Viewed from a contextual perspective, this text deals with a very specific historical situation related to the social practices of women at that time. An accurate translation is "I don't allow a wife to teach or to control her husband. Instead, she should be a quiet listener" (1 Tim 2:12 CEB).

9

The text is descriptive of a contemporary problem in a particular family; it does not prescribe policy for every household. To put it simply, the person reading the text must always be asking: Is this statement a description or a command? This distinction between *descriptive* and *prescriptive* applies to many biblical commands. Most of you have made the decision, for example, that commands related to cutting your hair or growing a beard are descriptive and not prescriptive in scripture. So the apparent prohibitive claim here related to women must be understood as descriptive in light of clear biblical testimony to the equality of women elsewhere.

Likewise, St. Paul admonishes that "women should be silent in the churches" (1 Cor 14:34 NRSV). But the context, here again, and not the literal meaning of the words, must guide our understanding of the statement. This command does not stand alone. Paul had already given the exact same command to be silent twice in this passage. He told various individuals and groups who were disrupting worship to be silent. Most translations, however, obscure the parallelism in Paul's censure, making it appear that he is more punitive toward women. To see the symmetry of Paul's repetitive parallelism restored, we can translate the text (ironically in a more literal manner true to the Greek) as follows: "To those who speak in tongues be silent" (verse 28); "to the prophets be silent" (verse 30); "to the women be silent" (verse 34). It is dishonest to single out the command directed to the women and make it more of an absolute than the command given to those who speak in tongues or to the prophets. The primary concern of this text is the disorderliness of worship in Corinth, not the prohibition of women. Here is the context: "God isn't a God of disorder but of peace. As in all the churches of God's people, the women should be quiet during the meeting. They are not allowed to talk. Instead, they need to get under control" (1 Cor 14:33-34 CEB).

Additionally, these two circumstantial texts should not overshadow the many clear texts that support women as teachers, preachers, and leaders in the Bible. The biblical witness, as a whole, provides five strong arguments supporting the rightful status and role of women.

1. God called women as leaders and prophets in the Hebrew Scriptures.

2. Women had important roles in the ministry of Jesus in the Gospels.

3. The experience of Pentecost anticipated and authenticated women's preaching and prophetic ministries, as in the case of Philip's four daughters and Priscilla's teaching Apollos.

4. St. Paul's policy statement with regard to women's equality (Gal 3:28) establishes a prescriptive norm in which "there is no longer male and female; for all of you are one in Christ Jesus" (NRSV).

5. St. Paul's own practice affirmed women in ministry, for example, in Romans 16 where he describes Phoebe as a deacon of the church at Cenchreae and Junia as a woman prominent among the apostles.

The "traditional" view—that the practice of "homosexuality" is incompatible with Christian teaching—has a lengthy history. But the same thing could be said about the prohibitions related to women, all of which have been overturned in the minds of most

Methodists. Likewise, the same thing could be said about the issue of slavery, the injustice of which was challenged only in the nineteenth century. The change of perspective with regard to both women and slaves hinged on a reassessment of scripture. And this must be the case today with regard to "the LGBTQ+ question." Biblical literalists and many others base their judgments with regard to the status, role, and place of LGBTQ+ persons on a very limited number of biblical texts, which are read and used out of context: Leviticus 18:22, Leviticus 20:13, 1 Corinthians 6:9-10, 1 Timothy 1:10, and Romans 1:26-27. Obviously, some of these are single sentences in the Bible, while others, particularly the Romans text, are framed by a more extended narrative. Steve Harper provides one of the best discussions of these texts in *Holy Love*, based on his extensive examination of scholarly work in this arena. Rather than rehearse the arguments here, I leave it to you to consult that or other resources I have suggested at the conclusion of this book.

Steve Harper's conclusion, drawn from a close study of these texts, provides helpful instruction:

> When we put it all together, we see that the Bible is against sexual sin that is promiscuous, driven by excess passion, and abusive—any sexual behavior that shames others by treating them as objects rather than as people, any sexual behavior that subjugates another person and controls them for one's own self-gratification.[7]

Like the texts related to women, these passages are much more complicated than they appear. They do not lead to the conclusion that these siblings should be excluded from either fellowship or leadership in the life of the church.

One of the differences between the arguments for the inclusion of women in ministry and LGBTQ+ inclusion relates to the issue of positive evidence in scripture. The parallelism with regard to these two targets of discrimination breaks down at this point. Whereas scripture celebrates the historic leadership of women within the community of faith, no such explicit evidence elevates the status and roles of LGBTQ+ persons. In the absence of positive evidence, we must rely on what John Wesley called the "general tenor of scripture." The overarching narrative of scripture and its salient themes that reveal God's way (the whole), illuminated by the Holy Spirit, must guide the interpretation of difficult or ambiguous texts (the parts).

This principle dominates all other interpretive tools in Wesley's effort to understand God's Word. It applies all the more in the face of silence—with regard to questions the Bible does not fully address. Such, I believe, is the case with regard to the issue of LGBTQ+ inclusion. In the same way that Wesley continually refers to the general tenor of scripture to justify breaking rules or revising his interpretation of difficult passages, we can apply this principle to the case of our LGBTQ+ siblings. In his examination of John Wesley's conception and use of scripture, Scott Jones observes that "many particular texts, when taken literally, do not support the general tenor Wesley has found."[8] So how does the grand tenor of scripture apply to this issue?

An exploration of the three major themes of the biblical narrative related to love put into action provides a strong case for inclusion.

Creation or Re-Creation (purpose). God created all that is out of love. God loves all that God created. Despite the brokenness that characterizes our individual lives and our human family, God is at work to restore love's image in our lives through a process of re-creation. God wills that we reach out to another in love. And as Jesus confirms, "Whoever does the will of my Father who is in heaven is my brother, sister, and mother" (Matt 12:50 CEB). Love is every person's reason for being.

Covenant (relationship). God makes covenants with people that provide a structure for redemption. According to Steve Harper, four characteristics dominate the biblical conception of covenant: sacredness (holiness); fidelity (faithfulness); permanency (unending); and with regard to sexuality, monogamy (singular devotion). These characteristics apply to all relationships in life, regardless of their nature. God seeks to infuse these qualities into all relationships of love.

God's Reign (mission). Everything moves ultimately toward the realization of God's rule in all things. This is God's grand mission. The biblical vision of this reign is characterized by justice, peace, harmony, and love—shalom. Under the rule of God all persons are free to embrace and employ their unique gifts in partnership with God. Every person has a role to play in God's restoration of all things.

Given the general tenor of scripture, encapsulated in these themes, three things become immediately apparent with regard to our LGBTQ+ kin. Stated directly to these siblings:

1. You are beloved of God; love is your reason for being.

2. Your loving relationships can be expressed in sacredness, fidelity, permanency, and monogamy.

3. As beloved children of God you are invited to use your gifts to the fullest possible extent in the embodiment of God's vision of shalom.

Originally, John Wesley opposed women preachers. In fact, he stood in opposition even to laymen stepping into this role. When he left Thomas Maxfield in charge of the London Foundery Society, this layman overstepped his bounds and began preaching. Wesley returned hastily to put a stop to this. Susanna Wesley, however, who had witnessed his preaching, advised her son to listen to him before he intervened. He experienced Maxfield's gifts and saw the fruits of his labor. Thereafter, lay preachers became the foundation of his movement.

Likewise, this was the case with regard to the women. When several women preachers emerged in the life of the movement, this forced Wesley to take a look at the so-called prohibitive biblical texts afresh. They seemed to be so out of sync with his experience of this ministry. He came to believe God called the laywomen as well as laymen into this vocation. In the end, he welcomed women's ministry and became one of the women preachers' strongest proponents. Moreover, he made sure that those within Methodism honored the work to which God had called them. If God has called our LGBTQ+ siblings to this work and they display the gifts, graces, and fruit related to this ministry, who are we to stand in their way? Does this not require our reexamination of the biblical texts as well?

These two contemporary issues are critical in the life of the church today. A leader willfully lacks humility when claiming that the biblical texts about women or same-sex relationships

15

can only be read as prohibitions against sin. One claims exclusive possession of the truth. Another smacks of arrogance and intransigence. Instead of opening up channels of communication and dialogue, the literalist shuts the gate, closes the door, and essentially barricades oneself in a cocoon of self-certainty. Disdain of others follows immediately in its wake. Like the religious leader in Jesus's parable of the Pharisee and the tax collector, such a person prays, "God, I thank you that I'm not like everyone else" (Luke 18:11 CEB). And as you know, Jesus's story concludes: "All who lift themselves up will be brought low, and those who make themselves low will be lifted up" (Luke 18:14 CEB).

These contemporary illustrations of how fundamentalism, and particularly biblical literalism, distorts the mission and witness of Jesus should at least raise a red flag for us all. I believe that a progressive Wesleyan rediscovery of the practice of humility can help us break through this and other similar impasses.

Engaging in the Practice of Humility

Humble people lift others up; they don't knock others down. This virtue of humility can only be shaped in our lives through practice. Life in Christ is all about humility. And this quality of humility must extend to our claims about truth as well. This is the way of Jesus. If we practice humility, we enter into the journey of life in a very different posture, and that's the gift I want to offer you. So how can you practice humility in your daily walk?

The Prayer of Examen can be a wonderful practice in the formation of a spirit of humility. Ignatius of Loyola developed this practice as part of his famous *Spiritual Exercises*. It combines the need to examine your conscience with the issue of your consciousness of God in life. It involves reflection through five movements with regard to the day just lived.

Here are instructions for how you can apply humility with each step.

1. *Quiet yourself.* The Prayer of Examen begins with a celebration of life and an expression of thanks to God. Assume the posture of kneeling for this first movement. This actually puts you in a posture of humility before God.

2. *Seek illumination.* Pray for grace to see yourself clearly, in your humility before God and others and in your pride. Use a prayer like this one in this movement of the Examen: "Lord, teach me where and how to find you in the midst of my life. You always seek to lift up your children. You are at work for good in the world; so open my eyes to see you every day and to be like you."

3. *Examine your life.* Inventory the course of your day as if watching a video playback. Allow God to show you concrete instances in which you lifted other people up or knocked others down. Picture each person and how your words and actions impacted his or her life, either positively or negatively.

4. *Relinquish your brokenness.* Review your spiritual health with regard to the virtue of humility, and your need for forgiveness and healing. Pray the words of the psalmist:

   Examine me, God!
   Look at my heart!

17

> Put me to the test!
> Know my anxious thoughts!
> Look to see if there is any idolatrous way in me,
> then lead me on the eternal path!
> (Ps 139:23-24 CEB)

5. *Pray for forgiveness* for those situations in which you failed to lift others up when you had the chance.

6. *Embrace God's grace.* Give thanks to God for those circumstances in which you were able to lift other people up, even at great cost to yourself. Express gratitude to God for giving you the strength and courage to act in ways that were humble and kind. Live in the resolve that tomorrow is another day, with fresh opportunities to love and serve. You may close your time of Examen with a prayer like this one:

> Help me, Jesus, to model my life after your life of humility and service to others. Give me the strength and courage to lift other people up rather than knocking them down; for your sake and in your name, I pray. Amen.

Find truth in the practice of humility.

Discussion

1. What are the words and images of the ancient Christian hymn, Philippians 2:5-11, that stand out to you and linger in your mind? How have these shaped your understanding of what it means to be a follower of Jesus?

2. Have you ever engaged in conversation with someone who was fixed in his or her attitudes or way of thinking—unmovable? How did this make you feel? How did you deal with the situation?

3. The Wesleys made the distinction between "essentials" and "opinions" with regard to Christian truth. What is your list of essentials?

4. Describe a recent experience in which you intentionally "lifted someone up." How did this shape how you feel about yourself and how did it help you both grow into your full potential?

Chapter Two

JOY AND THE PRACTICE OF HOSPITALITY

When some people in the United States were stoking up fear against Muslims, my daughter, Anna, felt compelled to do something. The divisive and inflammatory rhetoric she was hearing every day unsettled her deeply. She had come to know a young Muslim woman at the gym and approached her after a workout. "I just wanted to see how you're doing with everything that's happening in the world today," she said. "I'm sure it's got to be hard, and I just want you to know you're not alone. I'm standing with you." They hugged and cried together. Saadia felt seen, heard, and loved. Together, they welcomed each other in friendship and took a leap of faith. They decided to bring their Muslim and Christian friends together—to provide a space for conversation and connection. So a simple act of kindness and hospitality launched a deep friendship that blossomed into a group they called "women in solidarity." Everyone experienced so much joy in what they were doing that the group expanded and further diversified. "It's about all of us," Anna says, "jointly growing together, understanding each other, nurturing relationship, growing in empathy, and working toward peace."

Hospitality has to do with creating safe space for others. Whenever we "make room," God blesses us with deep joy. That's what this chapter is all about, the practice of hospitality. Progressive Wesleyans invite others into the sacred space of faithful love.

Hospitality in Matthew 25:34-40

Jesus focuses much attention on the practice of hospitality. He demonstrates through his words and his actions that real victory in life comes not by conquering and consolidating power for your own group but by making yourself vulnerable. Moreover, he challenged the narrow definitions of hospitality in his own time. He made room for those with whom most would never have sought any kind of connection, let alone a relationship. Instead of avoiding the "other," Jesus made those "others" his friends and companions. He used those relationships to illustrate the character of his way. All this comes to something of a climax in his story of the great judgment in Matthew 25:

> Then the king will say to those on his right, "Come, you who will receive good things from my Father. Inherit the kingdom that was prepared for you before the world began. I was hungry and you gave me food to eat. I was thirsty and you gave me a drink. I was a stranger and you welcomed me. I was naked and you gave me clothes to wear. I was sick and you took care of me. I was in prison and you visited me."
>
> Then those who are righteous will reply to him, "Lord, when did we see you hungry and feed you, or thirsty and give you a drink? When did we see you as a stranger and welcome you, or naked and

give you clothes to wear? When did we see you sick or in prison and visit you?"

Then the king will reply to them, "I assure you that when you have done it for one of the least of these brothers and sisters of mine, you have done it for me." (Matt 25:34-40 CEB)

Christine Pohl, in her study of the practice of hospitality, *Making Room*, describes the significance of this singular text:

> This has been the most important passage for the entire tradition on Christian hospitality. "I was a stranger and you welcomed me" resounds throughout the ancient texts, and contemporary practitioners of hospitality refer to this text more often than to any other passage. Acts of welcoming the stranger, or leaving someone outside cold and hungry, take on intensely heightened significance when it is Jesus himself who experiences the consequences of our ministry or the lack of it.[1]

God's commands about the care of strangers, immigrants, and the neglected and rejected of society pervade the scriptural witness. The author of Deuteronomy makes this all about love in the shared human experience of feeling alone, of not belonging: "That means you must also love immigrants because you were immigrants in Egypt" (Deut 10:19 CEB). The book of Leviticus contains clear statements about hospitality: "Any immigrant who lives with you must be treated as if they were one of your citizens. You must love them as yourself, because you were immigrants in the land of Egypt; I am the LORD your God" (Lev 19:34 CEB). Here again, the empathetic response of the faithful depends in some measure on the way in which they have experienced oppression themselves. Chapter 58 in the prophecy of Isaiah addresses the issue of false and true worship. True worship, the prophet claims, means "sharing your bread with the hungry, and bringing the homeless poor into your house" (verse 7). For those who obey the way of the Lord in this regard, "your light will shine in the darkness" (verse 10). The lives of those who offer hospitality are filled with joy.

The New Testament reiterates this theme repeatedly. St. Paul admonishes the Christian community in Rome quite simply, "Contribute to the needs of God's people; and welcome strangers into your home" (Rom 12:13). The most remarkable passage related to hospitality comes from a later epistle. "Keep loving each other like family," writes the author of the letter to the Hebrews. "Don't neglect to open up your homes to guests, because by doing this some have been hosts to angels without knowing it. Remember prisoners as if you were in prison with them, and people who are mistreated as if you were in their place" (Heb 13:2-3 CEB).

A poignant story illustrates how a couple took this admonition to heart. Jürgen Moltmann is well known for a "theology of hope." I first met Professor Moltmann when I was a graduate student at Duke University. During one of his visits to campus, I invited him to lunch and we enjoyed a wonderful meal together. While introducing myself to him more fully, I explained that I was working in my doctoral studies with Frank Baker. "Oh," he interrupted, "I'd like to share a story with you about Frank and Nellie Baker."

He said that during the war there was a camp for German prisoners on the northeast coast of England. A young pastor and his wife served a small Methodist circuit close by. They were filled with compassion and compelled to do something to reach out to these men. So they went to the commander and asked permission to take a prisoner with them to church each Sunday and then to their home, where they would eat their Sunday dinner together. It was agreed. So Sunday after Sunday, a steady flow of German soldiers worshiped and ate with the Bakers in their home throughout the course of the war. This world-famous theologian paused, looked at me intently, and said, "One of those soldiers was a young man by the name of Jürgen Moltmann. It was at Frank and Nellie Baker's dinner table that the seed of hope was planted in my heart."

Hospitality in Le Chambon-sur-Lignon

The mentor in hospitality you will meet in this chapter is not an individual; it is a small Christian village. Le Chambon-sur-Lignon, along with other nearby communities, provided refuge for thousands of people fleeing Nazi persecution, the vast majority of whom were Jewish children. Between 1940 and 1944, this little Protestant community under the leadership of Rev. André Trocmé and his wife, Magda, provided the refugees, mostly children, with food, shelter, and sanctuary. Everyone had to work together so as to avoid any suspicion. Protecting these new friends that they took into their homes as their own kin became the primary concern of the people. Trocmé had a reputation for having said, "You shall love the Lord your God with all your heart, with all your mind and with all your strength and love your neighbor as yourself. Go practice it."[2] After the war, when one of the villagers was asked why they had done what they did, he simply said, "Because it was the right thing to do."[3] Magda Trocmé echoed,

25

"There was no decision to make. The issue was: Do you think we are all brothers or not? Do you think it is unjust to turn in the Jews or not? Then let us try to help!"[4] A village modeled hospitality in the way of Jesus.

The early Methodist people were known for their hospitality as well. Mary Bosanquet moved to a poor and depressed area of London called Leytonstone to care for the poor, neglected, and marginalized neighbors she had befriended there. She gathered around her a community of young women to share in this ministry. After much careful deliberation the women decided to take in none but the most destitute and hopeless. Over the course of five years, they sheltered and cared for thirty-five children and thirty-four women. They modeled for others what can only be described as a progressive Wesleyan spirit.

John Wesley described their "experiment" as one of the most exemplary developments within his movement. He kept this model Christian community, combining vibrant personal piety and active social service, under his personal surveillance. On February 12, 1767, he was so delighted by his discoveries that he exclaimed, "O what a house of God is here! Not only for decency and order, but for the life and power of religion! I am afraid there are very few such to be found in all the king's dominions."[5] All accounts emphasize the fact that the primary characteristic of this community was joy.

Henri Nouwen, in his devotional classic entitled *Reaching Out*, describes three important movements in the spiritual life. One of these movements involves a transformational journey from hostility to hospitality. I am still drawn to one of his particularly poignant statements:

> Our society seems to be increasingly full of fearful, defensive, aggressive people anxiously clinging to their property and inclined to look at their surrounding world with suspicion, always expecting an enemy to suddenly appear, intrude and do harm. But still—that is our vocation: to convert the *hostis* into a *hospes*, the enemy into a guest and to create the free and fearless space where brotherhood and sisterhood can be formed and fully experienced.[6]

Progressive Wesleyan Christians seek to turn enemies into friends by making room for them in their lives and in their communities.

The Danger of Nationalism

"Christian" nationalism is one of the most dangerous distortions of the way of Jesus in our time. It is antithetical to the practice of hospitality. This is not the first time, of course, that elements within a society have advanced a nationalistic agenda. We can go as far back as the Egyptian pharaohs. Fearing for the ethnic uniformity and survival of their kingdom, given the increasing number of the Israelites among them, they resorted to murder to consolidate their power (Exod 1). National Socialism in Germany following the First World War led to one of the most vicious forms of nationalism in modern history. Whenever people unite around their own race, particular ethnic group, or nation and assume an antagonistic posture toward others, nothing good ever comes out of it.

We can trace the origins of nationalism, like fundamentalism, to a basic human need and a fear. People thrive when they have a sense of belonging. The need to belong is another of Maslow's primary needs in the hierarchy he developed. You need a community you can call your own, and this is good. But this basic need can get turned in unhealthy directions. Studies show, for example, that a sense of belonging more than any other reason leads youth in urban settings to join gangs. So even on a local level, an "us versus them" mentality dominates the logic of nationalism.

Throughout human history, people have naturally gravitated toward those who look, speak, and think alike. But nothing more than fear stirs up and establishes a nationalistic spirit. This fear has to do with feeling overrun, with losing your sense of identity given the diversity surrounding you on every side. We want our nation to be great; again, not a bad thing in itself. But if a form of American nationalism or ideology that privileges one group—or idealizes a "golden age" of white privilege—becomes the narrative that defines your life, you have sacrificed the gospel. The narrative of God's concern about and love for all people no longer defines your life. An idolatrous love of nation squeezes out your love for Jesus and his way. A host of other "isms" press into our lives when we assert the priority of my people, my way, my nation.

Racism emerges often as nationalism's closest ally. Sometimes—as is the case in our own time—nationalistic leaders permit the resurgence of dormant racist attitudes because they promote their agenda. Reawakened, racism emerges, wreaking havoc and destroying relationships. "We/they" rhetoric fills the air. Racist scapegoating provides simplistic solutions to complex

28

problems. Unfortunately, these protectionist attitudes infiltrate the church. Jonathan Wilson-Hartgrove, in his prophetic study *Reconstructing the Gospel*, explains how the practice of owning slaves in American history, for example, subverted our reading of the Bible. He argues cogently that if we are to be freed from institutional racism, we must embrace a Christianity that recognizes the equal worth of every person. In an era of resurgent racism, aligned with nationalism, our faith demands that we engage in this hard work. In an interview with William Barber, he offered this glimmer of hope: "On the other side of the work," Wilson-Hartgrove claims, "there's a great freedom and joy—the joy that's there in the beloved community."[7]

Nativism is the policy of protecting the interests of native-born or established inhabitants against those of immigrants. Nationalism frequently moves in this direction as well. Two instances drawn from the history of the United States must suffice. Just prior to the American Civil War, the opponents of Irish, German, and Catholic immigration in the United States founded the Order of the Star Spangled Banner. To become a member of this nativist organization you had to be at least a twenty-one-year-old Protestant willing to do whatever the leaders of the Order told you to do without question. These American nativists believed that the "alien riffraff" would displace white Protestantism and seize their power.

Later, at the end of the nineteenth century, several Harvard alumni founded the Immigration Restriction League aimed at restricting the immigration of southern and eastern Europeans, including 2.5 million Ashkenazi Jews who entered the United States after fleeing pogroms and murder between 1880 and 1918. The anti-immigration leagues considered people from these regions to be inferior to those coming from Anglo-Saxon stock. They argued that these newcomers threatened the American way of life and would bring increased poverty and crime at a time of economic hardship for many. Eventually, by 1924 opponents to immigration had persuaded Congress to prohibit further immigration from races they considered inferior and illiterate. Even as America was defining quotas and erecting barriers at ports of entry, nationalism and fascism were plunging the world into economic collapse. It ended in violent chaos with the deaths of more than 60 million people.

Does anything change?

Xenophobia—the fear of others—provides the foundation for almost all forms of nativism, racism, and nationalism. This fear always sows seeds of discord, threatens peace, divides communities, and ultimately robs people of joy. The recent recurring cancer of this fear in the United States can be traced, perhaps, to the time of the American bicentennial in 1976. This nostalgic era gave rise to a desire among some to preserve an exceptional "American identity" that, in their minds, seemed to be disappearing. Conservative Christians, in particular, feared the compromise of cherished traditional or family values that defined, so they believed, the United States as a Christian nation. The so-called "culture wars" ensued. White evangelicals engaged in efforts to "win America back." In her trenchant study of the rise of Christian nationalism in America, *Kingdom Coming*, Michelle Goldberg demonstrates how this particular form of nationalism has been able to make such deep inroads in our national life. Not only supported by entrenched theological and ideological dogmas, the right-wing evangelical culture aligned with these developments has been buoyed by political patronage in hopes of stemming the tide of change.

A former colleague and biblical scholar, Dan Hawk, posted this timely statement on July 1, 2019:

> It seems to me that the decline of American Christianity's influence can be attributed, in large part, to its determination to respond to societal change not by loving more intentionally and intensely, but by doubling down on doctrinal boundaries and moral dictates. In so doing, we have become just another angry voice vying for influence in the political arena. We have been seduced by the notion that Christianity is essentially an ideology, rather than an intricate web of relationships binding us to our Lord and to others.

I think he is absolutely right.

Nationalism, and its xenophobic symptoms of racism and nativism, I contend, is antithetical to the way of Jesus. Love of country so easily devolves into exclusive loyalty to my tribe. Patriotism, when motivated by fear, can become a force for animosity and hatred aimed at any person you perceive to be a threat to your own power or privilege. The progressive Wesleyan vision, rooted in scripture and the Christian practice of hospitality, offers an alternative to this form of idolatry.

Contemporary Concern: Immigration

The flashpoint for these concerns today is the issue of immigration, at a time when more than 65 million people worldwide are migrating to flee violence and deprivation. This battle against an evolving culture of diversity convinced millions of Christians in the United States to ignore the uniform witness of scripture about welcoming the stranger. Instead, Christian nationalists embrace nativist attitudes in their fear of the others coming to our shores or borders.

This issue continues to divide the nation and the church. In *Seeking Refuge*, three experts from World Relief, an evangelical humanitarian organization, describe the global refugee crisis as the greatest geopolitical issue of our time. They offer a compelling portrait of the plight of refugees and the extraordinary opportunity we have to love our neighbors as ourselves. One of the authors, Matthew Soerens, teamed up with Jenny Yang to publish *Welcoming the Stranger*, a resource demonstrating how to overcome the violence, poverty, and injustice associated with immigration through an active faith. They examine the complexities of the immigration issue from many angles, but the primary contribution they make is to put a human face on the issue. They tell the stories of immigrants and the struggle of families seeking asylum in the United States. They debunk myths and misconceptions about immigration, which are often invoked as facts, by nativists in order to incite fear and opposition. Ultimately, they identify how the principle of hospitality can inform immigration reform that is compassionate, sensible, and just, while navigating all the complex issues that revolve around this crisis.

It should be no surprise that white evangelicals, in particular, consistently favor harsh and punitive actions related to immigrants. A survey on this topic, published by the Public Religion

Research Institute, demonstrated that 57 percent of white evangelicals believe immigrants threaten American society.[8] No other religious group in the United States makes such a claim. More than half support banning refugees from entering the United States. Against their "build a wall, keep them out, protect ourselves" mentality, The United Methodist Church has long maintained a policy of hospitality. The "Rights of Immigrants" section of the Social Principles (approved in 2008) states:

> We recognize, embrace, and affirm all persons, regardless of country of origin, as members of the family of God. We affirm the right of all persons to equal opportunities for employment, access to housing, health care, education, and freedom from social discrimination. We urge the Church and society to recognize the gifts, contributions, and struggles of those who are immigrants and to advocate for justice for all. We oppose immigration policies that separate family members from each other or that include detention of families with children, and we call on local churches to be in ministry with immigrant families.

More recently, in the face of extreme "separation of family policies," the Council of Bishops joined other church leaders in the Americas to voice its indignation. Their "Joint Statement in Response to the Central American Migrant Caravans" reads, in part:

> We call upon President Donald Trump to cease characterizing our migrant brothers and sisters in derogatory and fear-inducing ways, castigating them as criminals when in fact they have the right under International Law to seek asylum. As the leader of the most powerful and wealthiest nation in the world, we call him forth to lead with truth, justice and moral compassion.
>
> Above all, we call upon our congregations to be agents of God's mercy toward the migrant.[9]

33

One of my former students from Duke Divinity School, Gavin Rogers, made the bold decision to join the Central American Caravan to see for himself exactly what was happening. I followed his posts with great interest as he made the arduous journey north with hundreds of refugees. "It is a long road," he wrote on November 11, 2018. "But life is good when you are with people filled with love and hospitality." Countering the lies and deceptive images associated with nativist propaganda (some of which have been endorsed by highly visible evangelical leaders such as James Dobson), he observed that "the love these families have for each other is outstanding." Echoing the sentiments of a progressive Wesleyan vision, the motto of Rogers's church is "unconditional love and justice in action."

From the experience of his solidarity with those who were hoping to seek asylum in the United States, he took away six lessons.

1. They welcomed a stranger with open arms.

2. They wanted to be known and seen.

3. They didn't want more than the essentials.

4. Their struggle didn't end when they got to the border.

5. Christians responded more negatively than he expected.

6. The migrants taught him empathy—and they can teach others, too.[10]

Progressive Wesleyan Christians seek to make room for others—whether they are those seeking asylum from violence and death, LGBTQ+ folks who are marginalized and ostracized, or anyone who looks, speaks, or acts differently—and to learn from them.

Engaging in the Practice of Hospitality

Hospitable people build bridges; they don't build walls. In his award-winning book, *Exclusion and Embrace,* Miroslav Volf explores contemporary concerns related to identity, otherness, and reconciliation. As a Croatian by birth, with firsthand experience of the attempted "ethnic cleansing" in former Yugoslavia, he considers xenophobia to be the most disturbing reality of our time. If Christians are to have a credible witness today, he argues, they must find the courage to address the hatred that people feel with regard to the "other." The concept of embrace, he believes, provides a most promising response to the problem of exclusion. The simple anatomy of an embrace teaches important lessons about the nature of hospitality. Volf describes its four basic elements: opening the arms, waiting, closing the arms, and opening them again.[11]

1. Opening my arms communicates both discontent and desire. Reaching out to you says that I am not content to be by myself. I want you to be a part of who I am, and I desire to be a part of who you are as well.

2. Waiting sends the signal that I do not want to impose myself on you. I respect your boundaries. I cannot coerce an embrace or it destroys the purpose of the welcome. An embrace requires mutuality and reciprocity.

3. Closing my arms leads to an amazing paradox. In the embrace I am being held and I am holding you. You are

35

being held and you are holding me. I must be careful not to overpower you; you must attend to my interests in the same way.

4. Opening my arms again culminates the embrace. Neither you nor I lose our unique identity in an embrace. We return to ourselves. But I carry the trace of your presence with me, and you carry me with you. The gift of the embrace encourages, empowers, and renews.

I suggest a practice that, while not a hug, mimics the anatomy of an embrace. Think for a moment about people in your near proximity who are different from you. Perhaps you have wondered about them? What do they believe? What is their story? How might your life be enriched by reaching out to them, as Anna did to the young Muslim woman she had seen?

Identify one of these persons in your own world and extend a simple invitation to coffee for a conversation. Start out at a high comfort level. A neighbor might be a good place to begin. When you meet at the appointed time, if you have not done so already, you might say, "I am just wanting to get to know people around me better. I'd simply love to hear your story."

Wait, then, and listen attentively. You will be amazed by the stories you hear and how anxious that person is to share his or her story with you. Reciprocate by saying something about yourself. A half-hour conversation can change you.

Smile and express your appreciation for the time you have been able to spend together. You have shared sacred space. Be honest. Be genuine and authentic. You cannot inflict harm by saying thank you. This is like closing your arms in an embrace.

Then part company. After you have had an opportunity to reflect on the experience, write down your thoughts. How did the conversation make you feel? What did you learn? How has the encounter changed you? At some point in the days that follow, write a handwritten note of thanks to the person you have come to know more fully. In your letter, identify one or two discoveries that have helped you.

Consider the possibility of practicing this coffee conversation on a regular basis. Shift the "level of the comfort bar" as you advance. Perhaps there are others within arm's reach who are different from you in obvious ways. A person of a different race or ethnic group, religion, sexual orientation or identity?

Reach out. Offer an invitation. Talk. Learn. Grow. Open your heart to those around you who are different. Do all you can to be an agent of reconciliation who partners with God to transform enemies into friends. As my dear friend Peter Storey said to me one day, "When we sing 'Come into my heart, Lord Jesus,' he replies, 'Only if I can bring my friends.'" That is Jesus's way.

Find joy in the practice of hospitality.

Discussion

1. How has Matthew 25 shaped your life? Describe situations in which you have found Jesus in the people he has called you to serve.

2. Describe a situation in which someone offered hospitality to you. How did it make you feel?

3. Who are the "others" in your life and what do you fear about them? How do these fears shape your view of immigration questions?

4. Describe a recent situation in which you offered hospitality to someone or made room for someone "at your table." How did it make you feel? What did you discover?

Chapter Three

PEACE AND THE PRACTICE OF HEALING

I was mesmerized. For five minutes I was glued to the screen. I was watching an amazing short documentary entitled *How Wolves Change Rivers* with a group of United Methodist clergy.[1] The idea was that this documentary, based on the reintroduction of wolves to Yellowstone National Park in 1995, would trigger conversations about change in the church. How could a film on an ecological process known as a trophic cascade capture such attention? Well, here's the story.

By the mid-1990s wolves had been absent from Yellowstone for seventy years. During that period of time, the deer population increased exponentially. They grazed away the vegetation, leading to a thoroughgoing ecological destabilization. The simple restoration of wolves to the park, however, had an opposite and remarkable effect. They killed some of the deer, of course, but more importantly they changed the deer's behavior. Deer avoided those areas of the park that were now dangerous. The valleys and gorges began to regenerate. The height of the trees actually quintupled in just six years. Forests emerged from prairies once stripped bare. Birds returned and filled the trees. The ecosystem engineers of nature—the beavers—built dams. They re-created habitats for other creatures. Rabbits and mice multiplied. Other species—from carrion to rodents, from predatory birds to bears— repopulated the park. Not only did the restoration of the wolves transform the park, it actually changed the behavior of the rivers. They stopped meandering and stagnating. Their channels narrowed and flowed more freely. The banks of the rivers no longer collapsed, because they were stabilized by regenerated forests. The wolves changed the rivers and recovered the ecosystem. They restored life to Yellowstone.

These next two chapters focus on two different but interrelated aspects of a central Wesleyan theme: restoration. This chapter deals with God's command to care for the world; chapter 4 addresses the issue of personal salvation as restoration. Ask yourself this question as you read this chapter: What is my role in the healing of the world? To be sure, this issue demands your immediate attention. While multifaceted, two specific dimensions of the healing of creation have reached a tipping point: climate change and human discord. Both have to do with the restoration of harmony in the face of abuse and violence. If we do not get our response to the first of these concerns right, then nothing else in this book really matters. We have a very limited window of opportunity to restore the integrity of creation. The second dimension—animosity and violence toward one another—parallels the human abuse of our earthly home. We need to be actively involved in healing our world in this arena as well.

Healing has to do with recovery and restoration. Whenever you engage in the practice of healing in the world, you connect with the peace that God intends. Progressive Wesleyans seek to partner with God in this work of recovery.

Healing in Isaiah 11:6-9 and 2 Corinthians 5:17-20

A wide variety of biblical texts shapes this vision of peace, healing, reconciliation, and restoration. Scripture repeatedly defines God's purpose in terms of healing and recovery. Biblical writers from the prophets to Jesus and Paul provide a vivid portrait of God's goal—the "peaceable reign" or the "kingdom of God." No Hebrew writer articulates this vision more poignantly than the prophet Isaiah. The prophet provides his iconic vision of a renewed harmony in all creation in Isaiah 11:6-9:

> The wolf will live with the lamb,
>> and the leopard will lie down with the young goat;
>> the calf and the young lion will feed together,
>> and a little child will lead them.
> The cow and the bear will graze.
>> Their young will lie down together,
>> and a lion will eat straw like an ox.
> A nursing child will play over the snake's hole;
>> toddlers will reach right over the serpent's den.
> They won't harm or destroy anywhere on my holy mountain.
> The earth will surely be filled with the knowledge of the LORD,
>> just as the water covers the sea. (Isa 11:6-9 CEB)

Jesus uses all these images and embodies the peaceable reign in his own life and ministry. His acts of healing, nurturing, and reconciliation function not as a mere prelude to his work of redemption on the cross but constitute the core of his mission. "Before Jesus embarks on his ministry of healing and reconciliation, he declares that this harmony between himself and the Creator is about to be restored through the whole earth (Mark 1:14-15)."[2] This is his mission, and all creation groans in anticipation of God's rule, which reconciles and restores.

St. Paul goes to great lengths to emphasize the centrality of this vision of shalom to Jesus's mission. Those drawn into this realm love both God and neighbor. Christ makes this kind of existence possible by breaking down all the barriers that divide people and disrupt God's intended harmony throughout creation. Reconciliation itself reveals God's presence and the nearness of God's rule. "Amidst the world's profound brokenness," writes a leader in reconciliation studies, "God's peace in the risen Christ is now powerfully at work, seeking to reconcile humanity to God's intended purposes for union with God, one another, and the material creation, resulting in the flourishing of all."[3]

Jesus's mission, in fact, points to a much larger vision of redemption than most Christians tend to imagine. St. Paul understood this. Neither Jesus nor Paul limits his understanding of salvation to the experience of individuals. St. Paul's language of "new creation" in 2 Corinthians 5:17 expands our vision of redemption to the whole universe. Older English translations of this verse tend to obscure the more radical nature of this vision. John Wesley picked up on this. In his *Explanatory Notes upon the New Testament* he deviates from the King James Version—"Therefore if any man be in Christ, he is a *new creature*." Rather, Wesley suggests, "Therefore if anyone be in Christ, there is a *new creation*." His exposition of the verse explores the breadth of Paul's meaning: "he lives, as it were, in a new world. God, men, the whole creation, heaven, earth, and all therein, appear in a new light."[4]

Richard Hays offers direct rendering of the Greek syntax: "If anyone is in Christ—new creation." Through Jesus, God inaugurates a whole new realm of shalom: "So then, if anyone is in Christ, that person is part of the new creation" (2 Cor 5:17 CEB). The implications that surround these biblical insights are profound. Hays continues:

> Once the church has caught the vision of living as a sign of the new creation in which racial and ethnic differences are bridged at the table of the Lord, how it is possible for the community of Christ's people to participate in animosity toward "outsiders"? If God is the creator of a whole world who wills ultimately to redeem the whole creation…then how can the church that is called to bear God's message of reconciliation in an unredeemed world (2 Cor. 5:17-20) scorn or reject people of any race or tongue, whether they are Christians or not?…The church has the task of embodying "the ministry of reconciliation" in the world.[5]

Restoration means participation in the story of God's loving mission. That story of God's mission, into which we are drawn, goes something like this:

God sings all that is into existence and declares its goodness. Human action harms both the natural world and the world of human relationships and disrupts the original harmony of creation. Determined to restore humankind and all creation, in the fullness of time, Jesus enters human history to continue God's mission of recovery. His most radical innovation is the commitment to refrain from violence even at the expense of his own life and the success of his mission. God vindicates the way of Jesus in bringing life from death and invites the whole human family to partner

43

with Christ—the risen Lord—through the power of the Spirit in this mission of shalom. God calls those within the community of faith to be ambassadors of reconciliation and peace—to pray and to work for the restoration of God's rule through acts of faithful love and through the care for our common home.

St. Paul declares in Romans 8:22-23 that all creation groans in labor pains as we await the completion of God's good work of restoration.

John Wesley described this more holistic view of salvation as the restoration of all creation. In his sermon "The New Creation," he encouraged his followers to strive toward that day when "there will be a deep, an intimate, an uninterrupted union with God...and of all the creatures in him!"[6] Early Methodists devoted their energies toward the realization of God's beloved community. They addressed the environmental concerns of their own day, like open sewers, polluted air and water, and substandard housing. They sought to be agents of reconciliation, mediating conflicts among their neighbors and finding ways to bring peace to their communities. They lived in solidarity with the poor, engaged in compassionate action, challenged injustice, and waged peace. Through all these actions, God's reign broke in upon them and gave them a glimpse of the goal of shalom to which they were committed.

Healing in St. Francis of Assisi

The life of St. Francis of Assisi provides one of the most compelling portraits of a disciple of Jesus committed to God's mission of peace and healing. He is our mentor in this practice. Some Franciscans have dubbed their founder the patron saint of ecology. Of his namesake, Pope Francis claims he is "the example par excellence of care for the vulnerable and of an integral ecology lived out joyfully and authentically."[7] St. Francis carried these twin concerns for God's creation throughout his life and ministry. He attempted to live in harmony with nature, others, and God. He sought to restore harmony to everyone and everything around him through what he called "apostolic poverty" and simplicity. Moreover, he demonstrated the inseparable bond between the care of God's world and all God's children in the way of peace.

St. Francis lived the image of restoration articulated by Isaiah and manifested in Jesus. His "Canticle for the Sun" sings about the harmony he experienced with the natural world:

> Be praised, my Lord, through all your creatures,
>   especially through my Brother Sun;
> Be praised, my Lord, through Sister Moon and the stars;
> Be praised, my Lord, through Brothers Wind and Air,
>   and clouds and storms;
> Be praised, My Lord, through Sister Water;
> Be praised, my Lord, through our sister Mother Earth;
> Be praised, my Lord, through those who forgive for love of you.

In his "Peace Prayer" he taught us how to pray so as to embody the values of God's beloved community—to provide a living portrait of God's vision of shalom for others:

> Where there is hatred, let me sow love;
> where there is injury, pardon;
> where there is doubt, faith;
> where there is despair, hope;
> where there is darkness, light;
> where there is sadness, joy.

45

He reminds us that the broken world—characterized by hatred, injury, doubt, despair, darkness, and sadness—is not what God intends. Rather, God desires the community of faith to live before this world with a vision of life characterized by love, pardon, faith, hope, light, and joy. What a legacy St. Francis hands on to us. What a challenge. What an adventure filled with possibility and hope.

The key to his joy-filled life can be found in his commitment to each and every creature as a sister and a brother united to him by the bonds of love. Because of the love he had experienced in Christ, he felt compelled to care for all that exists. Pope Francis describes the motivation of his actions and the dangers of failing to heed his example:

> Such a conviction cannot be written off as naive romanticism, for it affects the choices which determine our behaviour. If we approach nature and the environment without this openness to awe and wonder, if we no longer speak the language of fraternity and beauty in our relationship with the world, our attitude will be that of masters, consumers, ruthless exploiters, unable to set limits on their immediate needs.[8]

St. Francis demonstrates for us the possibility of a restored creation. He postures himself in life as a healer—an agent of God's presence to restore and make new.

Throughout Christian history many have risen to God's challenge to partner in this work. The Social Gospel Movement within Methodism emphasized the way in which God was at work to realize peace with justice—shalom—in human history. The "social gospelers"—spiritual forebears of progressive Wesleyans today—sought to reclaim the centrality of the "kingdom of

God" in Christian theology and practice. They were unwavering, like the Wesleys, in their refusal to separate personal religion from social witness and action. They called for nothing less than a theological reconstruction of the church. The current mission statement of The United Methodist Church—"to make disciples of Jesus Christ for the transformation of the world"—echoes their concerns.

Hymns played a huge role in the communication and implementation of these ideas. Contemporaries aptly described the social gospel songs as "we" rather than "I" hymns—"this-worldly" in their orientation rather than "other-worldly"—concerned just as much about the redemption of the social order as individuals. The hymn writer Frank Mason North championed this cause. "Where Cross the Crowded Ways of Life" reflects his passion for the healing and restoration of the world. He articulates the Social Gospel yearning for the new Jerusalem. He appeals to everyone to learn the way of Jesus—the way of loving service—until the kingdom of God comes. He frequently drew people's attention to that phrase of the Lord's Prayer, often repeated but less frequently embraced: "Thy kingdom come *on earth* as it is in heaven." He prays for healing and restoration:

> O Master, from the mountainside
>> make haste to heal these hearts of pain;
>> among these restless throngs abide;
> O tread the city's streets again.
>>> till all the world shall learn your love
>>>> and follow where your feet have trod,
>>> till, glorious from your heaven above,
>>>> shall come the city of our God!

47

"This hymn has but one mission in the world," North observed in later years, "and that is to help [people] of all races and conditions better to understand the person and meaning of Jesus Christ."[9]

Progressive Wesleyan disciples understand that Jesus came not only to save us from our sins but for us to partner with God in the restoration of the world. They embrace God's invitation into that mission. They seek to heal the brokenness that characterizes the human family and to repair the damage done to the material creation. They care passionately for our planet and for all others in the human family.

The Danger of Dispensationalism

In their book *Healing All Creation*, Connell and Bartholomew describe the origins of "dispensationalism," one of the most dangerous distortions of the biblical vision of restoration in our time.

> In the nineteenth century, a dystopian worldview far different from the peaceable kingdom of Isaiah's prophecy took hold of the Christian imagination: a doomsday scenario of an evil world full of misguided people who are eventually destroyed by an angry God. The few righteous souls who escape destruction are "raptured," taken up into heaven for a life of eternal bliss.[10]

John Nelson Darby formulated this pessimistic and defeatist view of the end-times based on a literalistic interpretation of isolated scriptural texts taken out of context. Despite the fact that his ideas directly contradict the grand biblical vision of God's mission of restoration, over the past half century they have become increasingly popular—considered "gospel"—in some quarters of the church.

C. I. Scofield modified and popularized this apocalyptic vision in the United States. After the First World War his chain reference Bible became the best-selling annotated Bible in history. By being held in such high esteem, many assumed its authority without questioning the dispensationalist view of God and human history it contained. By the middle of the twentieth century Hal Lindsey further popularized Darby's interpretations of scripture, especially his dire, apocalyptic vision associated with Israel. He gained an immense following of young Christians who were both enthralled and terrified by his novel *The Late, Great Planet Earth.* Tim LaHaye and Jerry Jenkins continued the trend with their Left Behind series of novels. Connell and Bartholomew lament how "the appeal of this worldview endures today among self-identified Christians who prefer predetermined judgments and a punitive gospel of fire and brimstone to the compassionate healing actions of Jesus."[11] The apocalyptic or dystopian plots of movies and television dramas today further exacerbate the problem.

So why is this insurgent ideology so dangerous? It fixates people's attention on the end-times and diverts their attention from ministry here and now. It focuses on personal salvation from sin through Jesus, a self-interest that leaves little time for or interest in compassion and justice in this world. It leads to an escapist view of redemption antithetical to the life-affirming theology of the Bible. It limits Christian vocation to evangelism and ignores God's mandated mission to care for the world. As N. T. Wright claims in *Surprised by Hope*, it creates a false division between saving souls and doing good in the world, seeing value only in the former.[12] According to Howard Snyder, it reinforces the divorce between earth and heaven, a nonbiblical perspective that has plagued authentic Christianity for centuries. As the title of his study on God's project of global restoration declares: Salvation Means Creation Healed.[13]

So dispensationalism promotes passivity, detachment, apathy, and escapism. A progressive Wesleyan vision promotes action, engagement, and involvement in the care of both our human family and our earthly home.

Contemporary Concern: Climate Change

Dispensationalist theology leads some Christians today either to deny the reality of climate change or to disregard it as a superfluous concern about a world "going to hell in a hand basket." Unfortunately, we have operated for far too long under the delusion that there are no limits to our power and no consequences to our actions. We have looked upon the natural world simply as a resource to plunder, manipulate, and abuse. Connell and Bartholomew issue this potent warning:

> The urgency of our current environmental crisis—climate change, extreme weather, pollution, and mass extinction of species—warns us not to ignore the importance of the story of Jesus for our responsibility to our natural environment. The relentless focus on the afterlife has blinded us to our responsibilities to preserve and protect the environment and the spiritual richness of the natural world.[14]

Climate change presents one of the greatest challenges in human history. According to the landmark *Special Report on Global Warming*, published by the Intergovernmental Panel on Climate Change (IPCC) of the United Nations in October 2018, we have a little over a decade to reverse the global trends leading to a potential climate change catastrophe. The future of all life on this planet hangs in the balance.

Across the wide spectrum of Christian faith and practice, visionary leaders have spoken up to address the crisis we face—a crisis not only of ecological disaster but of human disharmony. The encyclical of Pope Francis, *Laudato Si*, released in June 2015, remains one of the most poignant statements on Christian responsibility for the care of creation and our common home. Pope Francis demonstrates the way in which our care for each other, our care for nature, and our spiritual life are inseparably linked. It is only by opening ourselves to hear the cry of the earth and the cry of the poor, he maintains, that we can make the changes we need. He calls all people to action to work toward change to protect our common home. Moreover, the encyclical makes dramatically clear how the violence we perpetrate upon nature goes hand in hand with the violence we perpetrate on our brothers and sisters in the human family.

The United Methodist Bishop's pastoral letter, *God's Renewed Creation*, published in 2009, expresses hope in the midst of a lament about three contemporary threats:

Our neglect, selfishness, and pride have fostered:

- pandemic poverty and disease,
- environmental degradation, and
- the proliferation of weapons and violence.

Despite these interconnected threats to life and hope, God's creative work continues. Despite the ways we all contribute to these problems, God still invites each one of us to participate in the work of renewal. We must begin the work of renewing creation by being renewed in our own hearts and minds. We cannot help the world until we change our way of being in it.[15]

God continues to call us to faithful love in action. God continues to invite us to embrace the mission inaugurated by Christ—a mission that recovers both the integrity of creation and the harmony of the human family. Care for creation offers a vision of hope:

> United Methodists are called to a ministry of reconciliation between God, humankind and creation. In and alongside frontline communities experiencing environmental injustices, we are participating in God's healing of creation. Through acts of personal, social and civic righteousness, United Methodists are modeling a new lifestyle and advocating for God's people and God's planet so that all God's children can share in the goodness of Creation.[16]

All faithful Wesleyans engage in the practice of healing as God's agents in the mission to restore the original harmony of creation. The urgency of this cause leaves no room for complacency. It calls for every ounce of your energy, to pour your efforts into the recovery and restoration of God's world. Jesus entered human history for something more than purchasing our tickets to heaven; rather, he came to restore all things. He calls you to be a healer and reconciler in his way. Jesus calls all creation, in fact, into God's unfolding reign of shalom. This is why you are here; this is why *we* are here.

Engaging in the Practice of Healing

Healers restore things; they don't wound and destroy. Progressive Wesleyans are not indifferent to anything in this world. But what can one person do? In the early 1960s, award-winning mathematician and meteorologist Edward Lorenz used the term "butterfly effect" to describe how a tiny action can generate big consequences. He discovered that the flapping of a butterfly wing on one side of the planet could affect the weather patterns on the other side of the earth. That principle can guide us here as well. Small actions we take can have monumental consequences. I believe that.

So here is a suggestion related to the practice of healing our world. I invite you to either make an individual covenant or, even better, form an "Earth Care" group for accountability around seven concrete actions. They all begin with the letter *R*. So you can remember them easily. Practice these daily, and at the end of each week take stock of how well you have done and where you can improve in your care of God's creation.

I/we promise to...

Refuse—to buy things I do not need.

Reduce—what I feel I must have.

Reuse—everything I possibly can.

Recycle—all items that can be refurbished for further use.

Rot—(that is compost waste) to return biodegradable items to the earth.

53

Rest—every week to reduce driving and shopping, and to enjoy God's creation.

Reform—the attitudes and behavior of others through information, advocacy, and political action.

All these practices are important and can make a big difference. Press onward through them. But don't forget how urgent the need is for immediate reform. Jim Patterson[17] quotes United Methodist pastor Mark Y. A. Davies, a widely respected expert on faith and ecology: "Unless we change the systems," Davies observes, "the economic system, the transportation system, energy system, the political system—we're not going to get to where we need to be in the amount of time we have left to get there." Take a stand politically today to heal our world, thereby waging peace.

Find peace in the practice of healing.

Discussion

1. How do the biblical images in this chapter affect you, especially Isaiah 11 and 2 Corinthians 5? Discuss what they stir up in you.

2. In a United Methodist prayer we affirm, "All day long God is at work for good in the world." Describe a situation in which you caught glimpses of God at work to make shalom real.

3. Is the idea of salvation as restoration and as something more than a personal relationship with Jesus new to you? If yes, how do you feel about this expansion of your vision of redemption?

4. Do you have specific ideas about how individuals and the Christian community can partner with God in the care of the world? What are you currently doing to help restore our planet?

Chapter Four

LOVE AND THE PRACTICE OF HOLINESS

Social reformer and women's rights activist Anna Howard Shaw was with her colleague, Susan B. Anthony, on their way to a women's suffrage event. They encountered a problem at the train station, potentially delaying their arrival. Shaw seized an opportunity and hopped on a train going in the opposite direction, leaving her bewildered colleague standing on the platform. When they met up at the event venue, Shaw said that she would rather be actively pursuing an alternative possibility than simply standing still. She was a woman of action.

This final chapter focuses on restoration and action in the life of the Christian disciple. The practice of holiness involves putting faith into loving action. It affirms the timeless insight of James: "Faith without actions has no value at all" (2:20 CEB). St. Paul makes the same claim in writing to the Galatians: "The only thing that counts is faith expressing itself through love" (5:6 NIV). While teaching Wesleyan theology, I often identify a gold thread running throughout the history of Methodism—the conviction that faith must be translated into action. How you conceive the

57

relationship between what you believe and how you live defines your understanding of what it means to follow Jesus. Rather than a lofty theoretical concept, I am describing:

how you live each day;

how you relate to the people around you;

what your faith in Jesus actually means;

in real time, with real people, in real life situations.

A pressing question emerges from this: How do God's love and holiness find expression in your life?

This is a deeply personal question, and the world needs a progressive Wesleyan vision of personal salvation as restoration. By progressive here I mean moving forward toward a goal—personal, relational, and dynamic—which revolves around growth in grace and love as it is lived out in life. Have you encountered a passive and static version of the Christian faith? Instead of filling you up with truth and joy and peace and love, are you hungry and thirsty? Never fear! You can feast on love and the Wesleyan vision for holiness of heart and life.

I met Brother Mark in Nairobi at Jomo Kenyatta Airport. He was scheduled to provide a weeklong spiritual life retreat at St. Paul's United Theological College, the seminary where I was teaching. We had never met before, so I wasn't quite sure what to expect. I had no picture, no description, only the ascetic image of a monk in my mind. I had been told quite simply that he was arriving on a flight from London Heathrow. And then he appeared, emerging from the baggage hall in his black cassock and large, black, wide-brimmed hat. "You must be Brother Mark?" I inquired cheerfully. "I am," he replied. "And what is your name, my dear young friend?" We were fast friends indeed. The journey to Limuru was nearly an hour, but I felt that I knew Mark immediately, and that I was immediately known. He exuded love. His words were filled with grace. His presence was uplifting. A voice deep down inside me said, "Jesus must have been like this." He loved to talk, and I was eager to listen to anything he had to say.

He describes the three selves in every person: the exterior self, the present self, and the true self. Brother Mark affirms that only genuine love can set us free to become our true self. This is the mystery that is you.[1] He offers a clear, even passionate, concern. He longs "for us to become mature adults—to be fully grown, measured by the standard of the fullness of Christ" (Eph 4:13 CEB). He often describes this process—the integration of all our "selves" into the gracious and loving purposes of God—like the growth of a flower. We do not push ourselves, he would say, we open ourselves into love. "Faith in Christ gives us a secure foundation," he affirms, "but the goal of life is to become a genuinely loving person. God created us to love. Jesus shows the way. The Spirit gives the growth." I immediately knew that this was the life for me.

In chapter 3 we explored the global arena of God's restorative work in the world and our partnership in that mission. But John and Charles Wesley also conceived salvation or redemption as restoration in the life of the believer. I intentionally present these two dimensions of restoration—the cosmic and the personal—in what most would consider to be given in the reverse order.

Many, perhaps most, Christians would address personal salvation first before considering restoration in terms of God's global mission. Especially in the West we tend to put ourselves in the center of everything. But personal redemption can only be understood properly in the context of God's larger work.

So you are pondering some of the big-picture questions named above: How does God recover the real you? How does God help you find your way home? While longing for your true home, how do you get there? At the close of *The Last Battle* in The Chronicles of Narnia, C. S. Lewis says it so well: "I have come home at last! This is my real country! I belong here. This is the land I have been looking for all my life, though I never knew it till now."[2] So now it is time for you to "come further up, come further in!"

Holiness has to do with submitting yourself to a process of growth in grace that leads to the unimagined possibilities of love. Whenever you translate your faith into concrete acts of love, you discover your true identity as God's dearly loved child. God created you for this very purpose. Progressive Wesleyans strive for holiness of heart and life—the fullest possible love of God intertwined with the fullest possible love of others.

Holiness in Luke 15:11-24

Spiritual restoration and the power of love is poignantly portrayed in the longest of Jesus's parables, recorded at Luke 15:11-24. Jesus shares a story about a father and his two sons.[3] You know it well.

A young son has requested his inheritance, squandered all he has, and finds himself miserable, alone, starving, dying, lost. Stripped of dignity, value, and identity, the critical turning point in the story comes with these important words, "When he came to his senses" (Luke 15:17 CEB, NIV, NET). John Wesley may be unique in defining repentance as "true self-understanding." He apparently takes his definition from Jesus's parable. The prodigal "came to himself" (KJV). In the depth of his despair, he remembered who he was and to whom he belonged. But that rediscovery was a two-edged sword. On the one hand, he understood too well who he was in that moment. He realized how far he had strayed. He was overcome with a sense of guilt and shame. He understood exactly what it meant to lose the dignity of his sonship. And that discovery—that self-revelation—broke his heart. But on the other hand, he came to himself in the sense of acknowledging the one to whom he belonged, realizing that nothing could ever strip him of his primary and eternal identity. He would always be his father's son, regardless. His repentance was an act of contrition and a rediscovery of true identity.

And so, the prodigal begins the long journey home, with his well-rehearsed greeting of sincere humility and remorse—of hope: "Father, I have sinned against heaven and against you; I no longer deserve to be called your son" (verses 18 and 21). But he was overwhelmed by his father's response. What his father had longed for more than anything else was to see the face of the one he loved. So nothing could have prepared the prodigal for what he experienced in his father's arms, just in sight of his home. "Within this reborn relationship the father's gifts to his son only amplify his love, which

61

has never lessened, and reestablish the signs of filial dignity the son thought he had lost," observes Maurizio Compiani, "Just like Jesus with the paralytic of Capernaum (Child, your sins are forgiven," Mark 2:5), this father also gives back to his son his true identity."[4]

This portrait of conversion and responding love captures the essence of Henri Nouwen's insight: being the beloved expresses the core truth of our existence. "The Father is always looking for me with outstretched arms," he professes, "to receive me back and whisper again in my ear: 'You are my Beloved.'"[5] We do not know about the succeeding chapters in the life of the prodigal. But we can speculate, or at least hope, that the restored son opened his heart to an unfolding life of shared love. He gets caught up in something more glorious and beautiful than he could have imagined, not without its ups and downs, but glorious nonetheless. He not only receives the forgiveness of his father, he begins to grow into his true identity—the image of his father. Perhaps he even begins to resemble his father more and more, not so much in appearance but in terms of his father's spirit, compassion, and loving action.

Holiness in Charles Wesley

In his sermon "The One Thing Needful," Charles Wesley defines personal redemption as the "restoration of the image of Christ":

> The recovery of the image of God, of glorious liberty, of this perfect soundness, is the one thing needful upon earth. This appears first from the fact that the enjoyment of perfect freedom and health was the singular purpose of our creation. For to this end you were created, to love God; and to this end alone, even to love the Lord your

God with all your heart, soul, mind, and strength. But love is the very image of God. It is the brightness of God's glory. By love you are not only made like God, but in some sense one with God.[6]

In a lyrical paraphrase of Revelation 3:17, Wesley describes how the repentant child of God "gasps to be made whole."[7] Isn't that the deepest yearning of all our hearts? We need someone to take the broken pieces of our lives and refashion them into something beautiful. The theme of "love restored" pervades Charles's lyrical theology. He views this as God's most treasured promise—a life restored to perfect holiness or love. This process begins with the restoration of the heart, what Howard Thurman described as a "citadel" in which we nurture all our hopes and fears, hatreds and loves.[8] With a heart renewed, God can begin the work of restoring the image of Christ in us. Essentially this means the recovery of Christlike love. The concluding stanza of Wesley's signature hymn, "Love Divine, All Loves Excelling," celebrates this lofty goal:

Finish then thy new creation,
pure and sinless let us be,
Let us see thy great salvation,
perfectly restored in thee;
Changed from glory into glory,
till in heaven we take our place,
till we cast our crowns before thee,
lost in wonder, love, and praise!

Three primary themes characterize Wesley's vision of redemption. First, the Spirit restores the image of Christ in the believer. Holiness means *restoration*. Those whom God has restored become transparent to the love that re-creates them. Secondly, transformed disciples of Jesus will be like him. Holiness means

Christlikeness. Those who bear the image of Christ conform to him in heart, mind, and life. For Charles, this call to conformity to Christ defines the disciple—it characterizes the Christian who is altogether God's—and it also reflects God's promise. Thirdly, those who are fully conformed to the image of Christ shine to God's glory. Holiness means *radiance*. The shining lives of God's restored children have a critical evangelistic role in the unfolding of God's reign. Light attracts; those who radiate the love of God draw others into God's realm of shalom. What an inspirational vision of what life is meant to be![9]

God accomplishes this great work in the life of the believer through the indwelling of the Holy Spirit. The glorious liberty that accompanies the Spirit not only frees from sorrow, fear, and sin but also liberates those who follow Christ to love fully. Charles acknowledged a profound spiritual dynamic at work in those who pursue holiness earnestly. This process of sanctification—to use the proper theological term—involves an apophatic (emptying) and kataphatic (filling) rhythm. Christian spiritual writers use this language. God expels or purges the "old" from those who seek holiness and fills them with the "new." Wesley uses powerful poetic language to express these spiritual gifts. The Spirit consumes, blots out, erases, and drives out sins, removing all barriers that separate us from God; the Spirit floods, fills, immerses, imparts, restores—teaches us to love:

> And when we rise in love renewed,
> our souls resemble thee,
> an image of the Triune God
> to all eternity.[10]

64

In works such as *The Divine Conspiracy, The Great Omission*, and *Renovation of the Heart*, Dallas Willard claims that God's primary intention is for everyone to become a Christlike child. He describes the Western church's neglect of sanctification—this process of growth in love and Christlikeness—as the great omission of our age. Willard describes spiritual transformation into Christlikeness as "the process of forming the inner world of the human self in such a way that it takes on the character of the inner being of Jesus himself."[11] "Single-minded and joyous devotion to God and his will, to what God wants for us—and to service to him and to others because of him," he also writes, "is what the will transformed into Christlikeness looks like." With Charles Wesley and a host of other kindred spirits, he conceived God's gift of salvation not only in terms of forgiveness but also as sanctification, of holiness of heart and life. The primary goal of the Christian life is not forgiveness, as important as this is. The goal is transformation, the restoration of the image of Christ, having the "mind of Christ" and bearing the "fruit of the Spirit."

In conversation about these things with a student at Africa University, she said, "You know, I don't believe God intends us just to muddle through life, as if the forgiveness of our sins is as good as it gets. I think God really intends us to soar."

The Danger of Antinomianism

While in high school, I distinctly remember some unsettling conversations with an adult neighbor across the street. He attended worship on Sunday and Wednesday evenings. A Bible study met in his home. He thought of himself as nothing other than a devout follower of Jesus. But I have never encountered a more inveterate racist in my life. He hated black people with a passion. And here is the main point. He sensed no disconnect between his faith in Jesus and his bitter hatred of others. I asked him about it one day, and this was his reply: "I am saved by my faith in Jesus and none of that other stuff matters. I'm going to heaven." He had divorced his faith from any outward actions in his personal life. In his *Plain Account of Christian Perfection* John Wesley bristled at this perversion of authentic Christianity. It features prominently in his advice concerning a life of genuine love: "Beware of *solifidianism*, crying nothing but 'Believe, believe!'" He warned his followers about the danger of a faith that does not lead to love.[12]

The term *solifidianism* comes from one of the watch cries of the Protestant reformation—*sola fidei*, or faith alone. This view of the Christian life actually turns the means of salvation (faith or trust in Christ) into the goal. Whereas faith is meant to be a means to love's end, the solifidian makes faith an end in itself. This radical "faith alone" perspective often leads to *antinomianism* (from the Latin roots meaning "against law"). Nothing frustrated John Wesley more than this distortion of the gospel. Since you are saved by faith, so the argument went, you are no longer bound to the moral law. You do not need to be loving. Obedience to the law or a life of good works, in other words, has no role in salvation, or even in being a follower of Christ. In the end, you live your life in a way that does not resemble the way of Jesus. Your life becomes disconnected from what you say you believe. This distortion of the biblical vision of life in Christ is exceedingly dangerous. Whenever Wesley encountered it, he often responded with Jesus's statement recorded in Matthew 7:21: "Not everybody who says to me, 'Lord, Lord,' will get into the kingdom of heaven. Only those who do the will of my Father who is in heaven will enter" (CEB).

Unfortunately, this view (more unconscious perhaps than openly affirmed) prevails among many Christians today. People claim to be Christians, but it is impossible for anyone to see the values of God's rule in their attitudes and actions. Rather than being like Jesus, they often exhibit lives diametrically opposed to Jesus's way. The contemporary issues you read about in this book illustrate this danger. Instead of humility, some Christians exude arrogance. Their attitudes and actions reflect their need or desire to "win" more than anything else. And politicians are quick to seize on the opportunity to exploit this weakness. Instead of hospitality, some Christians foment hostility. Their attitudes and actions clearly proclaim that "others"—whether LGBTQ+ kin or immigrants from south of the border—should keep their distance, stay away, go back home. Some people who claim to follow Jesus chant, "Build the wall" and "Send them back." Instead of healing, some inflict pain on others. Their attitudes and actions deny the harm we have done to the planet, the violence we have perpetrated against one another (particularly with guns), and the ways in which racism has defined our nation. The world finds it so hard to recognize Jesus in their attitudes or their actions and simply cries, "Hypocrites!"

Contemporary Issue:
A Two-Chapter Gospel

A misguided conception of redemption also undergirds this dangerous insurgency. "For most of Christian history," claim Connell and Bartholomew, "the default version of how humankind engages with God went something like this: Jesus came to Earth and died for my sins so that after I die, my soul can go to heaven and be with God forever."[13] Perhaps you know this version of the gospel through the "four spiritual laws" that were taught by Campus Crusade for Christ?

1. God loves you and offers a wonderful plan for your life.

2. All of us sin and our sin has separated us from God.

3. Jesus Christ is God's only provision for our sin. Through him we can know and experience God's love and plan for our life.

4. We must individually receive Jesus Christ as Savior and Lord; then we can know and experience God's love and plan for our lives.[14]

Some theologians describe this "sin-and-plan orientation to salvation" as the "two-chapter gospel." Its most flagrant expression is conveyed through the phrase "a ticket to heaven." In this view of salvation, the story begins with the fall and our sinfulness. Given the premise that "all have sinned and fall short of God's glory"; as St. Paul writes in Romans 3:23-24, "they are now justified by his grace as a gift, through the redemption that is in Christ Jesus" (NRSV). God's narrative of redemption, in other words, comes to its climax in the story of Jesus the Redeemer. This pervasive two-chapter view of salvation truncates the gospel. Moreover, as Whelchel demonstrates in *All Things New*:

- It does not tell us about our true destiny.

- It does not tell us why we were created.

- It does not tell us about what we were created to do.

- It tends to overemphasize the individualistic aspects of salvation. Salvation becomes all about us.

- It becomes a gospel of sin management.

- It creates a sacred/secular divide.

- It tends to lead to an escapist view of redemption.[15]

This shortchanged version of the gospel excludes God's original plan for creation characterized by shalom, and it says nothing about God's future restoration of all things in which universal flourishing and wholeness, beauty and delight reign.

As a consequence of this deficiency, some Christian leaders such as N. T. Wright, Tim Keller, and Hugh Whelchel urge our rediscovery of a "four-chapter gospel." In my own way of thinking, this is a rediscovery of the Wesleyan (biblical) vision of redemption. A recovery of the full scripture narrative completely changes your view of salvation, your purpose, and your place in the world.

> *Chapter One—Creation* affirms the original goodness
> and harmony of all that God created. God's grand narrative begins in goodness, beauty, and love.

Chapter Two—Fall distorts, damages, and defaces God's original design as a consequence of human hubris. Personal, social, and cosmic discord ensue.

Chapter Three—Redemption through the work of the Triune God reconciles all things in Christ and resituates the redeemed in a community of grace and love.

Chapter Four—Restoration completes God's work of divine improvisation in which humanity participates in the recovery of goodness, beauty, and love.

God has given you an amazing vocation in life. You are called to partner with God in a mission to make all things new. You are God's ambassador of peace, reconciliation, and beloved community.

Van Bogard "Bogie" Dunn was best known as a New Testament scholar and phenomenal storyteller. The story he loved to tell the most was the Gospel of Mark. Each year he recited from memory all of Mark's Gospel. After his retirement, I witnessed him preach what would be one of his last sermons. It contained this poignant story, and this is my memory of what he said:

> Earlier in my life, whenever I met someone new, they would invariably ask me what I did for a living. More often than not, I would say something like, "I am a theologian." Or "I am a New Testament scholar." And I would watch their eyes glaze over. But now, in retirement, whenever I am asked this question, I say somewhat excitedly that I help people find their way home. That gets their attention, and they are anxious to learn what I mean. I tell them that following Jesus is all about homecoming. It has to do with finding your way home into the loving arms of the One who embraces you as a beloved child. Your task—your privilege—is to open yourself to the Spirit of Christ in such a way that you grow into your true identity. Home. God wants to welcome you home.

Dean Dunn's life bore witness to the fact that you are a beloved child of God. God not only has liberated you through Christ from the brokenness of your life but seeks to restore the fullest possible love in you through the indwelling of the Spirit. An abundant life of love awaits. Embrace it. This is your true home.

Engaging in the Practice of Holiness

Holy people love God and others as fully as possible. They love because they have experienced God's unconditional love first. They seek to translate their faith into action. Faith works by love in their lives, leading to holiness of heart and life.

The best way to practice holiness is to pray, immerse yourself in God's Word, and then put your spiritual learning into action. Prayer shapes a heart of peace deeply connected to God's love. Immersion in the Word orients your life to the way of Jesus. Combining prayer and Word provides amazing opportunities for growth in the direction of perfect love. One of the most popular forms of praying the Word today is known as *lectio divina*. It involves all three of these approaches to "living in" scripture. With the meaning "divine reading," the purpose of this ancient spiritual practice is to cultivate the ability to listen deeply to the God who speaks to us through the Word. It fosters a receptive, imaginative, and loving spirit. It also facilitates your movement into concrete actions. Classically, this discipline consists of four movements, *lectio* (reading), *oratio* (prayer), *meditatio* (meditation), and *contemplatio* (contemplation). After selecting a passage upon which to meditate, you move successively through each of these exercises.

I suggest a simplified version of this meditative technique oriented around the four simple words, *proclaim, picture, ponder, practice*. This adapted form of *lectio divina* moves intentionally from contemplation to action. It emphasizes the formation of a receptive spirit and the cultivation of holy, loving action.

Before anything else, pray for the presence and guidance of the Holy Spirit.

> *Proclaim*: Read the passage. I recommend that you actually read it out loud. It helps to actually hear the Word "proclaimed."

> *Picture*: Read the same text again, this time picturing yourself somewhere in the narrative. With which person do you identify? Where do you find yourself in the drama that is unfolding imaginatively before your eyes?

> *Ponder*: After a third reading of the text, ponder what these words might mean for you today. What insight have you gained about yourself, God, your neighbor? What significance do you attach to your discoveries given your recent experiences, relationships, concerns?

> *Practice*: Following a final reading of the passage, resolve to translate your experience in the meditation into action. What is God calling you to do with this today? What action is required? What does God require of you to be an ambassador of reconciliation and love throughout the course of the day?

Close your meditation with a prayer for God's help and support as you seek to be faithful.

I invite you to meditate specifically on the parable of the prodigal son (Luke 15:11-24) over the course of one week.

Day One: Read and meditate on the entire passage using the guideline. Then follow the same meditative procedure with regard to shorter segments of the story as follows:

Day Two: Luke 15:11-13 (self-centered living)

Day Three: Luke 15:14-16 (self-despair)

Day Four: Luke 15:17-19 (true self-understanding)

Day Five: Luke 15:20-24 (restoration)

Day Six: Meditate again on the full text.

Day Seven: Reflect generally on your experience. What have you learned about love and holiness? How have you sought to translate your insights into action?

Find love anew in the practice of holiness.

Discussion

1. With whom do you relate most closely in the story of the prodigal son? The prodigal, the father, the older brother, or the absent mother? How does this story shape your vision of God?

2. What does holiness mean to you? How have the ideas of holiness as happiness, love of God, and love of neighbor changed your thinking?

3. How do you tend to explain who you are to other people? What are the adjectives you would use to describe yourself? How does being a beloved child of God relate to these descriptors?

4. Where do you go from here? What are the next steps you want to take in order to be a child of God whose life is characterized by truth, joy, peace, and love?

A PROGRESSIVE WESLEYAN DECLARATION

I pray that the ideas upon which you have been reflecting and the practices in which you have engaged have formed truth, joy, peace, and love in your life. The core values of the progressive Wesleyan vision include the mandate to translate faith into action, to conform in attitude and action to the values of God's reign of shalom, and to grow in grace into the fullest possible love of God and others.

This vision and these critical commitments are compressed below in "A Progressive Wesleyan Declaration." My hope is that you will return to this statement often as a reminder of the Wesleyan way. If you study this book in a group, I highly recommend that you recite this statement together when you meet for conversation. The Declaration can also be used as well in corporate worship. Words have power. They shape us and give us our identity. So simply hearing these words and being reminded about these practices can further shape them in the core of your being. Hopefully you will find this Declaration to be both convicting and inspirational. It provides yet another way to practice the Wesleyan way of humility, hospitality, healing, and holiness.

With confidence in the promises of God,
 faith in Jesus Christ,
 and in the power of the Holy Spirit,
 we declare:

We find Truth in Jesus.
Being found in human form,
 he emptied himself of all but love.
Like him, we seek to lift people up,
 assuming a posture of servanthood among all.
We pray that our practice of humility
 helps to break down barriers of human hostility.

We find Joy in Jesus.
He made room for others
 and invited all people into the sacred space of love.
Like him, we seek to create safe spaces for others,
 turning enemies into friends.
We pray that our practice of hospitality
 helps build bridges and tears down walls.

We find Peace in Jesus.
He embraced a mission of love,
 caring for all and restoring God's world.
Like him, we seek to partner with God
 in the recovery of God's vision of shalom.
We pray that our practice of healing
 helps to restore peace with justice everywhere.

We find Love in Jesus.
He demonstrated the fullest possible extent
 of the love of God and neighbor.
Like him, we seek to live a life of faith
 working by love leading to holiness.
We pray that our practice of holiness
 helps others to discover their true identity
 as the beloved children of God.

**We embrace the holistic and all-inclusive vision
of God's restoration of beloved community.**

A WORD TO PROGRESSIVE WESLEYAN CHRISTIANS

Thank you for working through the material in this book. My hope is that you were able to voice a hearty "Amen" to this summary of what it means to identify as a progressive Wesleyan Christian. God calls us to be agents of reconciliation and faithful love in all we do. As Wesleyan people we have a vision of life in Christ that is holistic and robust. The practices I recommend here simply demonstrate the many ways in which God can form us into a truth-telling, joyful, peaceful, and loving community for the sake of the world. So I encourage you to immerse yourself in the spiritual disciplines that shape your faith and form Christ in the core of your being.

I am also interested in genuine dialogue with people who think and believe differently than I do. I hope you share this desire. I invite you into this conciliatory ministry of conversation and dialogue. In the late 1980s I was entering into a very critical ecumenical phase in my own journey and found a helpful book by Michael Kinnamon, *Truth and Community*. I benefited from his insights and guidance time and time again, especially as I engaged in conversation across cultures, ideologies, and theologies. He suggests ten guidelines for dialogue that I highly commend as you engage in conversation with fellow United Methodists during these difficult times or with other folks you find to be "on the other side of the divide."[1]

1. Allow the other partners in dialogue to define themselves, to describe and witness to their faith in their own terms.

2. Have a clear understanding of your own faith and present it with complete honesty and sincerity.

3. Acknowledge that genuine dialogue rests on a common devotion to truth.

4. Recognize that dialogue is between people and not just between different perspectives or ideological positions.

5. Be sure to dialogue with contemporary partners; things change, and the past may no longer be relevant in the present.

6. Be willing to separate essentials from nonessentials and to require agreement only on the former.

7. Do not require more agreement from your partners in dialogue than you require from members of your own community.

8. Interpret the faith of the dialogue partner in its best rather than in its worst light.

9. Deal openly with the hard issues as well as those on which easier agreement is possible.

10. Search for ways to turn the increased understanding achieved through dialogue into activities for renewal.

We stand together at a critical juncture. My prayer is that you and I are so rooted in love, having been shaped by a vital relationship with the Triune God, that we are a source of reconciliation, healing, and love to all around us. Let's set the bar high in this regard. Let's make Christlike love the very center of who we are and all we do. And remember, God's loving promises to us and all God's children are "Yes" and "Amen."

AN OLIVE BRANCH EXTENDED

I honestly believe that fundamentalism, nationalism, dispensationalism, and antinomianism, as I have defined these ideologies here, are distortions of the gospel of Jesus Christ. You may be deeply committed to one or more of these perspectives. If so, that puts me in a posture "over against" you that I really do not like or desire. But I acknowledge this nonetheless. I truly seek understanding more than anything else and sincerely hope for reconciliation—something only ever possible as a consequence of God's grace. I do not hate you. I pray often that I hate no person. If I am to be like Jesus in this life, then that means I am called to love. I confess that it is easy to love those with whom I agree. Love comes less quickly with regard to those who seem to be my opponents. That is true for us all. But if we have any hope of true dialogue it must begin in a place of honesty. So I have to begin by saying, in my view, that some of the attitudes, words, and actions associated with these ideologies and theologies have perpetrated deep harm on people. This reflects neither godliness nor the spirit of Christ.

In this book I put scripture at the center of the conversation. I believe with my church that scripture contains everything necessary for salvation. If something is not found in scripture, or cannot be proved by scripture, then I do not believe it should be made an article of faith or taught as essential to salvation. The claim to possess all truth moves nothing forward. The elevation of nation over the identity of every person as a beloved child of God demeans God's vision. Anything less than the fullest possible love lived out in a sustainable world falls short of God's glorious plan. If the goal toward which I move in life is anything other than the self-sacrificing love of Jesus, then I am nothing more than "a noisy gong or a clanging cymbal" (1 Cor 13:1 NRSV). Dangerous ideologies and misguided theologies displace the good news of God's love for all people with principles based on fear. I believe that the progressive Wesleyan perspective I offer here is more fully biblical—and I desire to present it in a loving spirit—in the spirit of Christ.

My wife taught me long ago that I cannot change anyone. Only the Spirit can do that. So my prayer is that you will seriously consider engaging in the practices offered in this book. I truly believe that practices open up spaces in our lives where God's Spirit can work most effectively. I genuinely hope that you find ways to cultivate truth, joy, peace, and love in your hearts. If the practices of humility, hospitality, healing, and holiness lead in that direction, praise God! I truly believe this can make a big difference in your life as it has and continues to make in mine. I want to be the kind of Jesus-follower who opens doors and windows so that the light of Christ can flood our lives.

FOR FURTHER READING

This simple reading list reflects some of the more important books that shaped my thinking around the primary themes of this book. I reference most of them in the narrative of each chapter, so I have organized them here accordingly. I highly recommend that you explore any of these resources as prompted by the Holy Spirit. This can also be an extension of the practices of humility, hospitality, healing, and holiness addressed in this book.

Truth & Humility

Paul W. Chilcote, *The Imitation of Christ*

Paul W. Chilcote, *The Methodist Defense of Women in Ministry*

David Gushee, *Changing Our Minds*

Steve Harper, *Holy Love: A Biblical Theology for Human Sexuality*

Michael Kinnamon, *Truth and Community*

George Marsden, *Fundamentalism and American Culture*

Joy & Hospitality

Michelle Goldberg, *Kingdom Coming: The Rise of Christian Nationalism*

Henri Nouwen, *Reaching Out*

Christine Pohl, *Making Room*

Matthew Soerens & Jenny Yang, *Welcoming the Stranger*

Miroslav Volf, *Exclusion and Embrace, Revised and Updated*

Jim Wallis et al., *Christians and Immigration*

Peace & Healing

Richard Bauckham, *The Bible and Ecology*

Joan Connell and Adam Bartholomew, *Healing All Creation*

Jürgen Moltmann, *The Coming of God*

Barbara R. Rossing, *The Rapture Exposed*

Howard A. Snyder, *Salvation Means Creation Healed*

N. T. Wright, *Surprised by Hope*

Love & Holiness

Richard Foster, *Prayer: Finding the Heart's True Home*

Henri Nouwen, *The Return of the Prodigal Son*

John Wesley, *A Plain Account of Christian Perfection* (ed. Chilcote & Maddox)

Hugh Whelchel, *All Things New: Rediscovering the Four-Chapter Gospel*

Dallas Willard, *The Divine Conspiracy*

Dallas Willard, *Renovation of the Heart*

NOTES

Preface

1. For many of you, the term "progressive Wesleyan" may be new. By progressive here I mean moving forward in an effort to address the serious social issues of our time with integrity and action. Certainly this term includes some of the political connotations associated with it in the North American culture and church, but I conceive the term as something much larger than national or ecclesial politics. By Wesleyan I mean those Christians who understand their active faith in Jesus through the lens of the life and witness of John and Charles Wesley. In my view, the two terms "progressive" and "Wesleyan" go together properly and represent a genuine perspective that has integrity. In general, "progressive Wesleyan" refers to Methodists who embrace a view of the Christian life that is respectful of others, inclusive of all people, ecologically and socially aware, and oriented toward love above all things.

1. Truth and the Practice of Humility

1. Paul W. Chilcote, *The Imitation of Christ: Selections Annotated & Explained* (Woodstock, VT: SkyLight Paths, 2012), 5. All quotations from the *Imitation* are cited from this edition.

2. Paul Collins, "The Ongoing Threat of Fundamentalism," La Croix, December 24, 2018, https://international.la-croix .com/news/the-ongoing-threat-of-fundamentalism/8957.

3. See the results of the Barna Group research presented in David Kinnaman, *UnChristian: What a New Generation Really Thinks about Christianity…and Why It Matters* (Grand Rapids: Baker Books, 2007).

4. Terry L. Johnson, *Case for Traditional Protestantism: The Solas of the Reformation* (Edinburgh: Banner of Truth, 2004), 23–27. See chapter 2, *Sola scriptura*.

5. I use this initialism in reference to the various forms of sexuality alongside the heterosexual sphere. It is my effort to be respectful and appropriate given the evolution in terminology related to sexuality in our time. I have also attempted to avoid the language of brother and sister, opting for siblings and kin, as much as possible.

6. For a more thorough treatment of both these concerns, see Paul W. Chilcote, *The Methodist Defense of Women in Ministry* (Eugene, OR: Wipf & Stock, 2017); and Steve Harper, *Holy Love: A Biblical Theology of Human Sexuality* (Nashville: Abingdon Press, 2019).

7. Steve Harper, *Holy Love: A Biblical Theology for Human Sexuality* (Nashville: Abingdon Press, 2018), 47.

8. Scott J. Jones, *John Wesley's Conception and Use of Scripture* (Nashville: Abingdon Press, 1995), 215.

2. Joy and the Practice of Hospitality

1. Christine D. Pohl, *Making Room: Recovering Hospitality as a Christian Tradition* (Grand Rapids: Eerdmans, 1999), 22.

2. Quoted in Philip Hallie, *Lest Innocent Blood Be Shed* (London: Michael Joseph, 1979), 170.

3. From *Weapons of the Spirit* (1989), adapted from the ninety-minute documentary produced by Bill Moyers.

4. Carol Rittner and Sondra Myers, *Courage to Care: Rescuers of Jews During the Holocaust* (New York: New York University Press, 1986), 102.

5. John Wesley, *The Works of John Wesley, Volume 22, Journal and Diaries, V (1765—1775)*, ed. W. Reginald Ward and Richard P. Heitzenrater (Nashville: Abingdon Press, 1993), 70.

6. Henri J. M. Nouwen, *Reaching Out: The Three Movements of the Spiritual Life* (New York: Doubleday, 1975), 46.

7. "Jonathan Wilson-Hartgrove: Reckoning with the Racist History of American Christianity," *Faith & Leadership*, May 1, 2018, https://www.faithandleadership.com/jonathan-wilson-hartgrove-reckoning-racist-history-american-christianity.

8. Cited in Ulrike Elisabeth Stockhausen, "Evangelicals and Immigration: A Conflicted History," Process (blog), March 18, 2019, http://www.processhistory.org/stockhausen-immigration/.

9. Council of Bishops, The United Methodist Church, Joint Statement in Response to the Central American Migrant Caravans, November 7, 2018, http://www.umc.org/who-we-are/joint-statement-in-response-to-the-central-american-migrant-caravans.

10. Madeleine Stix, "6 Things a Texas Pastor Learned from Traveling with a Group of Migrants," CNN, updated December 5, 2018, https://www.cnn.com/2018/12/05/us/texas-pastor-migrant-caravan-lessons/index.html.

11. Miroslav Volf, *Exclusion and Embrace, Revised and Updated: A Theological Exploration of Identity, Otherness, and Reconciliation* (Nashville: Abingdon Press, 2019), 142–50.

3. Peace and the Practice of Healing

1. You can view this amazing five-minute documentary at https://www.youtube.com/watch?v=ysa5OBhXz-Q.

2. Joan Connell and Adam Bartholomew, *Healing All Creation: Genesis, the Gospel of Mark, and the Story of the Universe* (London: Rowman & Littlefield, 2019), 17.

3. Chris Rice, *Reconciliation as the Mission of God: Christian Witness in a World of Destructive Conflicts* (Tacoma: World Vision International Peacebuilding and Reconciliation Department, 2005), 11.

4. John Wesley, *Explanatory Notes upon the New Testament*, 2 vols. (London: Bowyer, 1755; repr., Salem, OH: Schmul, 1975), 2:457–58.

5. Richard B. Hays, *The Moral Vision of the New Testament: A Contemporary Introduction to New Testament Ethics* (San Francisco: HarperSanFrancisco, 1996), 441.

6. John Wesley, *The Works of John Wesley, Volume 2, Sermons II (34–70),* ed. Albert C. Outler (Nashville: Abingdon Press, 1985), 510.

7. Pope Francis, *Laudato Si: On Care of Our Common Home,* ¶10. This second encyclical of Pope Francis (2015) critiques irresponsible abuses of the planet and human violence, calling upon all the peoples of the world to swift global actions of restoration.

8. Pope Francis, *Laudato Si,* ¶11.

9. Cited in Cynthia Pearl Maus, *Christ and the Fine Arts* (New York: Harper & Brothers, 1938), 739.

10. Connell and Bartholomew, *Healing All Creation*, 45.

11. Connell and Bartholomew, *Healing All Creation*, 46.

12. N. T. Wright, *Surprised by Hope: Rethinking Heaven, the Resurrection, and the Mission of the Church* (New York: Harper, 2008).

13. Howard A Snyder with Joel Scandrett, *Salvation Means Creation Healed: The Ecology of Sin and Grace* (Eugene, OR: Cascade Books, 2011).

14. Connell and Bartholomew, *Healing All Creation*, 44.

15. You can consult the full pastoral letter of 2009, "God's Renewed Creation: Call to Hope and Action," at http://hopeand action.org/main/wp-content/uploads/2010/03/Pastoral-Letter -Eng-Handout-2-col.pdf.

16. See Social Principles, ¶160; *The Book of Resolutions of The United Methodist Church* (Nashville: The United Methodist Publishing House, 2016).

17. Jim Patterson, "Urgency Needed to Combat Climate Change," *United Methodist News*, July 16, 2019: https://www.um news.org/en/news/urgency-needed-to-combat-climate-change.

4. Love and the Practice of Holiness

1. All this was fresh on his mind, as I later learned, as he had recently published these ideas in a book on prayer entitled *Love and Life's Journey: Venture in Prayer* (Oxford, UK: A. R. Mowbray, 1987).

2. C. S. Lewis, *The Last Battle* (London: Bodley Head, 1956), chapter 15.

3. See my discussion of the parable in *Changed from Glory into Glory: Wesleyan Prayer for Transformation* (Nashville: Upper Room Books, 2005), 60–61, upon which this material is based.

4. Maurizio Compiani, *Confession: The Sacrament of Mercy* (Huntington, IN: Pontifical Council for the Promotion of the New Evangelization, 2015), 27.

5. Henri J. M. Nouwen, *The Return of the Prodigal Son: A Story of Homecoming* (New York: Doubleday, 1992), 44.

6. Kenneth G. C. Newport, ed., *The Sermons of Charles Wesley* (Oxford: Oxford University Press, 2001), 365. I have modernized this paragraph to make it more accessible to the contemporary reader.

7. John and Charles Wesley, *Hymns and Sacred Poems* (Bristol, UK: Farley, 1742), 44.

8. For an extremely helpful discussion of these "issues of the heart," see The Arbinger Institute, *The Anatomy of Peace: Resolving the Heart of Conflict*, 2nd ed. (Oakland, CA: Berrett-Koehler Publishers), 2015.

9. I explore these images and ideas in two articles, "'All the Image of Thy Love': Charles Wesley's Vision of the One Thing Needful," *Proceedings of the Charles Wesley Society* 18 (2014): 21–40; and "Perfect Love Restored: The Language of Renewal in the Hymns of Charles Wesley," *Proceedings of the Charles Wesley Society* 22 (2018): [forthcoming].

10. Charles Wesley, *Hymns on the Trinity* (Bristol, UK: Pine, 1767), 58. Hymn 87:3. Slightly modernized.

11. Dallas Willard, *Renovation of the Heart: Putting on the Character of Christ* (Colorado Springs: NavPress, 2002), 159.

12. John Wesley, *Plain Account of Christian Perfection*, ed. Paul W. Chilcote and Randy L. Maddox (Kansas City: Beacon Hill Press, 2015), 136–40; question 34A.

13. Connell and Bartholomew, *Healing All Creation*, 117.

14. "Would You Like to Know God Personally?" CRU, accessed August 23, 2019, https://www.cru.org/us/en/how-to-know-god/would-you-like-to-know-god-personally.html.

15. Hugh Whelchel, *All Things New: Rediscovering the Four-Chapter Gospel* (McLean, VA: Institute for Faith, Work & Economics, 2016), 23–30.

Appendix A

1. For a full description of these guidelines, see Michael Kinnamon, *Truth and Community: Diversity and Its Limits in the Ecumenical Movement* (Grand Rapids: Eerdmans, 1988), 29–32.

Made in the USA
Columbia, SC
03 October 2023

23861246R00063